Abdelazer by Aphra Behn

OR, THE MOOR'S REVENGE.

Aphra Behn was a prolific and well established writer but facts about her remain scant and difficult to confirm. What can safely be said though is that Aphra Behn is now regarded as a key English playwright and a major figure in Restoration theatre

Aphra was born into the rising tensions to the English Civil War. Obviously a time of much division and difficulty as the King and Parliament, and their respective forces, came ever closer to conflict.

There are claims she was a spy, that she travelled abroad, possibly as far as Surinam.

By 1664 her marriage was over (though by death or separation is not known but presumably the former as it occurred in the year of their marriage) and she now used Mrs Behn as her professional name.

Aphra now moved towards pursuing a more sustainable and substantial career and began work for the King's Company and the Duke's Company players as a scribe.

Previously her only writing had been poetry but now she would become a playwright. Her first, "The Forc'd Marriage", was staged in 1670, followed by "The Amorous Prince" (1671). After her third play, "The Dutch Lover", Aphra had a three year lull in her writing career. Again it is speculated that she went travelling again, possibly once again as a spy.

After this sojourn her writing moves towards comic works, which prove commercially more successful. Her most popular works included "The Rover" and "Love-Letters Between a Nobleman and His Sister" (1684–87).

With her growing reputation Aphra became friends with many of the most notable writers of the day. This is The Age of Dryden and his literary dominance.

From the mid 1680's Aphra's health began to decline. This was exacerbated by her continual state of debt and descent into poverty.

Aphra Behn died on April 16th 1689, and is buried in the East Cloister of Westminster Abbey. The inscription on her tombstone reads: "Here lies a Proof that Wit can never be Defence enough against Mortality." She was quoted as stating that she had led a "life dedicated to pleasure and poetry."

Index of Contents

ARGUMENT

The old King of Spain, having conquered Fez and killed the Moorish monarch, has taken the orphaned prince Abdelazer under his protection and in time made him General. Abdelazer, though always courageous, has the desire of revenge ever uppermost, and to gain influence, rather than from any love, he becomes the Queen's paramour. She, being a lustful and wicked woman, joins with the Moor in poisoning her husband, at whose death Philip, her second son, newly returned victor from a martial expedition, leaving his army at some distance, rushes in mad with rage and publicly accuses his mother of adultery with Abdelazer. She is greatly incensed, but Cardinal Mendozo, as Protector of the King, promptly banishes her gallant. The young King Ferdinand, however, to please Florella, the Moor's wife, whom he loves, revokes this decree.

Abdelazer, in revenge, next orders his native officer Osmin to kill Philip and the Cardinal. They escape by night disguised as monks, whilst Abdelazer alarms the castle with cries of treason and tells the King that Philip and the Cardinal are plotting to murder him. Ferdinand orders Abdelazer to follow them, intending to visit Florella during her husband's absence. Abdelazer, fully aware of his plan, out of pride and mischief furnishes Florella with a dagger, bidding her stab the King if he persists in his suit. Elvira, the Queen Mother's confidante, Watches the King enter Florella's apartment and conveys the news to her Mistress who, with dissembled reluctance, informs Alonzo, the Moor's brother-in-law. Florella resists the King's solicitations and produces the dagger threatening to stab herself. At this juncture the Queen rushes in and, feigning to think that Florella was about to attempt the King's life, kills her. Her motive for this deed is, in reality, jealousy.

Whilst the King falls weeping at his dead mistress' feet Abdelazer enters, and in the ensuing fight Ferdinand is slain. Philip is then proclaimed King, but Abdelazer announcing he is a bastard, an avowal backed by the Queen, declares himself Protector of Spain, Overpowered by his following, The lords accept him. Alonzo, however, flies to Philip's camp with the tidings. A battle between the two parties follows, but the Queen treacherously detaches Mendozo, who loves her, from Philip, and although the Moors are at first beaten back they now gain the advantage and Philip is captured. At a general assembly of the nobles the Queen relates the false tale of Philip's illegitimacy and asserts that the Cardinal is his father. She privately bids Mendozo acknowledge this and so gain the crown, but he refuses to support the lie and is promptly arrested as a traitor. Abdelazer now brings forward the Infanta Leonora and proclaims her Queen of Spain, He next disposes of the Queen Mother by bidding Roderigo, a creature of his own, assassinate her forthwith. Roderigo gains admittance disguised as a friar and stabs her, upon which Abdelazer, to screen himself, rushes in and cuts him down. He next openly declares his love for Leonora and is about to force her when Osmin, his officer, enters to inform him that Alonzo, to whom Leonora is affianced, has resisted arrest but is at last secured. Abdelazer, enraged at the interruption, wounds Osmin in the arm. Leonora pities the blow; and the Moorish soldier, deeply hurt at the insult, resolves to betray his master. He accordingly goes to the prison where Philip, the Cardinal, and Alonzo are confined, and killing his fellow Zarrack who was to have been their executioner, sets them free. When Abdelazer enters he finds himself entrapped. He glories, however, in his crimes, and as they set on him kills Osmin, himself falling dead in the mêleé. The Cardinal is forgiven, Leonora and Alonzo are united, whilst Philip ascends the throne.

SOURCE

Abdelazer; or, the Moor's Revenge is an alteration of the robustious Lust's Dominion; or, the Lascivious Queen, printed 12mo, 1657, and then attributed to Marlowe, who was certainly not the author. It is now generally identified with The Spanish Moor's Tragedy by Dekker (Haughton and Day, 1600), although, as Fleay justly says, there is 'an under-current of pre-Shakespearean work' unlike either Dekker or Day. There are marked crudities of form and a rough conduct of plot which stamp it as of very early origin. Probably it was emended and pruned by the three collaborators.

Although often keeping close to her original, Mrs. Behn has dealt with the somewhat rude material in a very apt and masterly way: she has, to advantage, omitted the old King, Emanuel, King of Portugal, Alvero, father to Maria (Florella), and the two farcical friars, Crab and Cole; she adds Elvira, and whereas in Lust's Dominion the Queen at the conclusion is left alive, declaiming:

'I'll fly unto some solitary residence
When I'll spin out the remnant of my life
In true contrition for my past offences.'

Mrs. Behn far more dramatically kills her Isabella. Perhaps the famous assassination of Henri III of France by the Dominican, Jacques Clement, gave a hint for Roderigo masqued as a monk.

The sexual passion, the predominance of which in this tragedy a recent critic has not a little carpingly condemned, is entirely natural in such an untamed savage as Abdelazer, whilst history affords many a parallel to the lascivious Queen.

THEATRICAL HISTORY.

Abdelazer; or, The Moor's Revenge was first produced at the Duke's Theatre in Dorset Garden during the late autumn of 1677. It was supported by a strong cast, and Betterton, whose Othello, Steele—writing exquisitely in the Tatler, seems to have considered artistically quite perfect, was no doubt n wonderful representative of the ferocious Afric. The effective rôle of Queen Isabella fell to Mrs. Mary Lee, the first tragedienne of the day, Mrs. Marshall, the leading lady of the King's Company, having at this time just retired from the stage.

[Footnote: Her last rôle was Berenice in Crowne's heroic tragedy, The Destruction of Jerusalem (1677).] It is interesting to notice that Mrs. Barry on her way to fame played the secondary part of Leonora.

Abdelazer seems to have met with good success, and on Easter Monday, April, 1695, the patentees, after the secession of Betterton, Mrs. Barry, Mrs. Bracegirdle and their following to Lincoln's Inn Fields, chose the tragedy to reopen Drury Lane. The Moor was played by George Powell, a vigorous and passionate actor, who also spoke a new prologue written for the nonce by Cibber, then a mere struggler in the ranks. Colley's verses were accepted at the eleventh hour in default of better, and he tells us how chagrined he was not to be allowed to deliver them in person. The house was very full the first day, but on the morrow it was empty, probably owing to the inexperience of many of the actors and a too hasty rehearsing of the play.

On the stage Abdelazer was superseded by Edward Young's The Revenge, a tragedy largely borrowed in theme and design from Mrs. Behn, with reminiscences of Othello. Produced at Drury Lane, 18 April, 1721, with Mills, Booth, Wilks, Mrs. Porter and Mrs. Horton in the cast, it attained considerable success, and Zanga, the Moor, was long a favourite part with our greatest actors even down to the days of Kean, who excelled in it, and Macready. The Revenge is not without merit, and it stands out well before the lean and arid tragedies of its time, but this, unfortunately, is not much to say. It is not for a moment to be compared with the magnificent tapestry of Abdelazer, woven though the latter may be in colours strong and daring.

DRAMATIS PERSONAE

MEN

Ferdinand, a young King of Spain, in love with Florella.
Philip, his Brother.
Akdelazer, the Moor.
Mendozo, Prince Cardinal, in love with the Queen.
Alonzo, a young Nobleman of Spain, contracted to Leonora.
Roderigo, a Creature to the Moor.
Antonio, |
Sebastian, An Officer of Phillip's
Osmin, An Officer of Phillip's |
Zarrack, Moors and Officers to Abdelazer.
Ordonio, a Courtier.
A Swain, and Shepherds.

Courtiers, Officers, Guards, Soldiers, Moors, Pages, and Attendants.

WOMEN

Isabella, Queen of Spain, Mother to Ferdinand and Philip, in love with Abdelazer.
Leonora, her Daughter, Sister to Ferdinand and Philip.
Florella, Wife to Abdelazer, and Sister to Mrs. Betterton.
Alonzo.
Elvira, Woman to the Queen.
A Nymph, and Shepherdesses.
Other Women Attendants.

ABDELAZER; or, The Moor's Revenge

PROLOGUE

Gallants, you have so long been absent hence,
That you have almost cool'd your Diligence;
For while we study or revive a Play,
You, like good Husbands, in the Country stay,
There frugally wear out your Summer Suit,
And in Prize Jerkin after Beagles toot;
Or, in Montero-Caps, at Feldfares shoot.
Nay, some are so obdurate in their Sin,
That they swear never to come up again,
But all their Charge of Clothes and Treat retrench,
To Gloves and Stockings for some Country Wench:
Even they, who in the Summer had Mishaps,
Send up to Town for Physick for their Claps.
The Ladies too are as resolved as they,
And having Debts unknown to them, they stay,
And with the Gain of Cheese and Poultry pay.
Even in their Visits, they from Banquets fall,
To entertain with Nuts and Bottle-Ale;
And in Discourse with Secresy report
State-News, that past a Twelve-month since at Court.
Those of them who are most refind, and gay,
Now learn the Songs of the last Summer's Play:
While the young Daughter does in private mourn,
Her Lovers in Town, and hopes not to return.
These Country Grievances too great appear:
But cruel Ladies, we have greater here;
You come not sharp, as you are wont, to Plays;
But only on the first and second Days:
This made our Poet, in her Visits, look
What new strange Courses, for your time you took,
And to her great Regret she found too soon,
Damn'd Beasts and Ombre spent the Afternoon;
So that we cannot hope to see you here
Before the little Net-work Purse be clear.

Suppose you should have Luck
Yet sitting up so late, as I am told,
You'll lose in Beauty what you win in Gold:
And what each Lady of another says,
Will make you new Lampoons, and us new Plays.

SCENE Spain, and in the Camp.

ACT I.

SCENE I. A rich Chamber.

A Table with Lights, Abdelazer sullenly leaning his Head on his Hands: after a little while, still Musick plays.

SONG.

Love in fantastick Triumph sat,
Whilst bleeding Hearts around him flow'd,
For whom fresh Pains he did create,
And strange Tyrannick Pow'r he shewed;
From thy bright Eyes he took his Fires,
Which round about in sport he hurl'd;
But 'twas from mine he took Desires,
Enough t'undo the amorous World.

From me he took his Sighs and Tears,
From thee his Pride and Cruelty;
From me his Languishments and Fears,
And ev'ry killing Dart from thee:
Thus thou, and I, the God have arrri'd,
And set him up a Deity;
But my poor Heart alone is harm'd,
Whilst thine the Victor is, and free.

[After which he rouzes, and gazes.

ABDELAZER - On me this Musick lost? this Sound on me
That hates all Softness? What, ho, my Slaves!

Enter Osmin, Zarrack.

OSMIN - My gracious Lord

[Enter Queen Isabella, Elvira.

QUEEN ISABELLA - My dearest Abdelazer -

ABDELAZER - Oh, are you there? Ye Dogs, how came she in?
Did I not charge you on your Lives to watch,
That none disturb my Privacy?

QUEEN ISABELLA - My gentle Abdelazer, 'tis thy Queen,
Who 'as laid aside the Business of her State,
To wanton in the kinder Joys of Love
Play all your sweetest Notes, such as inspire
The active Soul with new and soft Desire,
[To the Musick, they play softly.
Whilst we from Eyes, thus dying, fan the Fire.
[She sits down by him.

ABDELAZER - Cease that ungrateful Noise.
[Musick ceases.

QUEEN ISABELLA - Can ought that I command displease my Moor?

ABDELAZER - Away, fond Woman.

QUEEN ISABELLA - Nay, prithee be more kind.

ABDELAZER - Nay, prithee, good Queen, leave me, I am dull,
Unfit for Dalliance now.

QUEEN ISABELLA - Why dost thou frown? to whom was that Curse sent?

ABDELAZER - To thee -

QUEEN ISABELLA - To me? it cannot be to me, sweet Moor?
No, no, it cannot, prithee smile upon me
Smile, whilst a thousand Cupids shall descend
And call thee Jove, and wait upon thy Smiles,
Deck thy smooth Brow with Flowers;
Whilst in my Eyes, needing no other Glass,
Thou shalt behold and wonder at thy Beauty.

ABDELAZER - Away, away, be gone

QUEEN ISABELLA - Where hast thou learnt this Language, that can say
But those rude Words. Away, away, be gone?
Am I grown ugly now?

ABDELAZER - Ugly as Hell

QUEEN ISABELLA - Didst thou not love me once, and swore that Heav'n
Dwelt in my Face and Eyes?

ABDELAZER - Thy Face and Eyes! Baud, fetch me here a Glass,
[To Elvira.

And thou shalt see the Balls of both those Eyes
Burning with Fire of Lust:
That Blood that dances in thy Cheeks so hot,
That have not I to cool it
Made an Extraction even of my Soul,
Decay'd my Youth, only to feed thy Lust?
And wou'dst thou still pursue me to my Grave?

QUEEN ISABELLA - All this to me, my Abdelazer?

ABDELAZER - I cannot ride through the Castilian Streets,
But thousand Eyes throw killing Looks at me,
And cry. That's he that does abuse our King
There goes the Minion of the Spanish Queen,
Who, on the lazy Pleasures of his Love,
Spends the Revenues of the King of Spain
This many-headed Beast your Lust has arm'd.

QUEEN ISABELLA - How dare you, Sir, upbraid me with my Love?

ABDELAZER - I will not answer thee, nor hear thee speak.

QUEEN ISABELLA - Not hear me speak! Yes, and in Thunder too;
Since all my Passion, all my soft Intreaties
Can do no good upon thee,
I'll see (since thou hast banish'd all thy Love,
That Love, to which I've sacrific'd my Honour)
If thou hast any Sense of Gratitude,
For all the mighty Graces I have done thee.

ABDELAZER - Do; and in thy Story too, do not leave out
How dear those mighty Graces I have purchas'd;
My blooming Youth, my healthful vigorous Youth,
Which Nature gave me for more noble Actions
Than to lie fawning at a Woman's Feet,
And pass my Hours in Idleness and Love
If I cou'd blush, I shou'd thro all this Cloud
Send forth my Sense of Shame into my Cheeks.

QUEEN ISABELLA - Ingrate!
Have I for this abus'd the best of Men,
My noble Husband?
Depriving him of all the Joys of Love,
To bring them all intirely to thy Bed;
Neglected all my Vows, and sworn 'em here a-new,
Here, on thy Lips
Exhausted Treasures that wou'd purchase Crowns,
To buy thy Smiles, to buy a gentle Look;
And when thou didst repay me blest the Giver?
Oh, Abdelazer, more than this I've done
This very Hour, the last the King can live,

Urg'd by thy Witch-craft, I his Life betray'd;
And is it thus my Bounties are repaid?
Whate'er a Crime so great deserves from Heav'n,
By Abdelazer might have been forgiven: [Weeps.
But I will be reveng'd by penitence,
And e'er the King dies, own my black Offence
And yet that's not enough, Elvira [Pauses.
Cry murder, murder, help, help.

[She and her Women cry aloud, he is surpriz'd, the Queen falls, he draws a Dagger at Elvira.

ELVIRA - Help, murder, murder!

ABDELAZER - Hell, what's this? peace, Baud 'sdeath,
They'll raise the Court upon me, and then I'm lost
My Queen, my Goddess. Oh raise your lovely Eyes,
I have dissembled Coldness all this while;
And that Deceit was but to try thy Faith.
[Takes her up, sets her in a Chair, then kneels.
Look up, by Heav'n,'twas Jealousy
Pardon your Slave, pardon your poor Adorer.

QUEEN ISABELLA - Thou didst upbraid me with my shameful Passion.

ABDELAZER - I'll tear my Tongue out for its Profanation.

QUEEN ISABELLA - And when I woo'd thee but to smile upon me,
Thou cry'st. Away, I'm dull, unfit for Dalliance.

ABDELAZER - Call back the frighted Blood into thy Cheeks,
And I'll obey the Dictates of my Love,
And smile, and kiss, and dwell for ever here
Enter Osmin hastily.
How now, why star'st thou so?

OSMIN - My Lord, the King is dead.

ABDELAZER - The King dead! 'Twas time then to dissemble. [Aside.
What means this Rudeness?
[One knocks.

Enter Zarrack.

ZARRACK - My Lord, the Cardinal inquiring for the Queen,
The Court is in an uproar, none can find her.

ABDELAZER - Not find the Queen! and wou'd they search her here?

QUEEN ISABELLA - What shall I do? I must not here be found.

ABDELAZER - Oh, do not fear, no Cardinal enters here;

No King, no God, that means to be secure
Slaves guard the Doors, and suffer none to enter,
Whilst I, my charming Queen, provide for your Security
You know there is a Vault deep under Ground,
Into the which the busy Sun ne'er enter'd,
But all is dark, as are the Shades of Hell,
Thro which in dead of Night I oft have pass'd,
Guided by Love, to your Apartment, Madam
They knock agen, thither, my lovely Mistress, [Knock.
Suffer your self to be conducted

Osmin, attend the Queen, descend in haste,
[Queen, Osmin and Elvira descend the Vault.
My Lodgings are beset.

ZARRACK - I cannot guard the Lodgings longer
Don Ordonio, Sir, to seek the Queen

ABDELAZER - How dare they seek her here?

ZARRACK - My Lord, the King has swounded twice,
And being recover'd, calls for her Majesty.

ABDELAZER - The King not dead! go, Zarrack, and aloud
Tell Don Ordonio and the Cardinal,
He that dares enter here to seek the Queen,
[Puts his Hand to his Sword.
Had better snatch the She from the fierce side
Of a young amorous Lion, and 'twere safer.
Again, more knocking!
[Knocking.

ZARRACK - My gracious Lord, it is your Brother, Don Alonzo.

ABDELAZER - I will not have him enter. I am disorder'd.

ZARRACK - My Lord, 'tis now too late.
Enter Alonzo.

ALONZO - Saw you not the Queen, my Lord?

ABDELAZER - My Lord!

ALONZO - Was not the Queen here with you?

ABDELAZER - The Queen with me!
Because, Sir, I am married to your Sister,
You, like your Sister, must be jealous too:
The Queen with me! with me! a Moor! a Devil!
A Slave of Barbary! for so
Your gay young Courtiers christen me. But, Don,

Altho my Skin be black, within my Veins
Runs Blood as red, and royal as the best.
My Father, Great Abdela, with his Life
Lost too his Crown; both most unjustly ravish'd
By Tyrant Philip, your old King I mean.
How many Wounds his valiant Breast receiv'd
E'er he would yield to part with Life and Empire:
Methinks I see him cover'd o'er with Blood,
Fainting amidst those numbers he had conquer'd.
I was but young, yet old enough to grieve,
Tho not revenge, or to defy my Fetters:
For then began my Slavery; and e'er since
Have seen that Diadem by this Tyrant worn,
Which crown'd the sacred Temples of my Father,
And shou'd adorn mine now - shou'd! nay, and must
Go tell him what I say, 'twill be but Death
Go, Sir, the Queen's not here.

ALONZO - Do not mistake me, Sir, or if I wou'd,
I've no old King to tell, the King is dead
And I am answer'd, Sir, to what I came for,
And so good night.
[Exit.

ABDELAZER - Now all that's brave and villain seize my Soul,
Reform each Faculty that is not ill,
And make it fit for Vengeance, noble Vengeance.
Oh glorious Word! fit only for the Gods,
For which they form'd their Thunder,
Till Man usurp'd their Power, and by Revenge
Sway'd Destiny as well as they, and took their trade of killing.
And thou, almighty Love,
Dance in a thousand forms about my Person,
That this same Queen, this easy Spanish Dame,
May be bewitch'd, and dote upon me still;
Whilst I make use of the insatiate Flame
To set all Spain on fire.
Mischief, erect thy Throne,
And sit on high; here, here upon my Head.
Let Fools fear Fate, thus I my Stars defy:
The influence of this must raise my Glory high.
[Pointing to his Sword.

[Exit.

SCENE II. A Room in the Palace.

Enter Ferdinand weeping, Ordonio bearing the Crown, followed by Alonzo, leading Leonora weeping; Florella, Roderigo, Mendozo, met by the Queen weeping; Elvira and Women.

QUEEN ISABELLA - What doleful Cry was that, which like the Voice
Of angry Heav'n struck thro my trembling Soul?
Nothing but horrid Shrieks, nothing but Death;
Whilst I, bowing my Knees to the cold Earth,
Drowning my Cheeks in Rivulets of Tears,
Sending up Prayers in Sighs, t' implore from Heaven
Health for the Royal Majesty of Spain
All cry'd, the Majesty of Spain is dead.
Whilst the sad Sound flew through the ecchoing Air,
And reach'd my frighted Soul. Inform my Fears,
Oh my Fernando, oh my gentle Son
[Weeps.

KING FERDINAND - Madam, read here the truth, if looks can shew
That which I cannot speak, and you wou'd know:
The common Fare in ev'ry face appears;
A King's great loss the publick Grief declares,
But 'tis a Father's Death that claims my Tears.
[Card. leads in the Queen attended.

LEONORA - Ah, Sir!
If you thus grieve, who ascend by what y'ave lost,
To all the Greatness that a King can boast;
What Tributes from my Eyes and Heart are due,
Who've lost at once a King and Father too?

KING FERDINAND - My Leonora cannot think my Grief
Can from those empty Glories find relief;
Nature within my Soul has equal share,
And that and Love surmount my Glory there.
Had Heav'n continu'd Royal Philip's Life,
And giv'n me bright Florella for a Wife,
[Bows to Florella.
To Crown and Scepters I had made no claim,
But ow'd my Blessings only to my Flame.
But Heav'n well knew in giving thee away, [To Florella.
I had no bus'ness for another Joy. [Weeps.
The King, Alonzo, with his dying Breath,
[Turns to Alon. and Leon.
To you my beauteous Sister did bequeath;
And I his Generosity approve,
And think you worthy Leonora's Love.

Enter Cardinal and Queen weeping.

ALONZO - Too gloriously my Services are paid,
In the possession of this Royal Maid,
To whom my guilty Heart durst ne'er aspire,
But rather chose to languish in its Fire.

Enter Philip in a Rage, Antonio and Sebastian.

PHILIP - I know he is not dead; what envious Powers
Durst snatch him hence? he was all great and good,
As fit to be ador'd as they above.
Where is the Body of my Royal Father?
That Body which inspir'd by's sacred Soul,
Aw'd all the Universe with ev'ry Frown,
And taught 'em all Obedience with his Smiles.
Why stand you thus distracted, Mother, Brother
My Lords, Prince Cardinal
Has Sorrow struck you dumb?
Is this my Welcome from the Toils of War?
When in his Bosom I shou'd find repose,
To meet it cold and pale! Oh, guide me to him,
And with my Sighs I'll breathe new Life into't.

KING FERDINAND - There's all that's left of Royal Philip now,
[Phil, goes out.
Pay all thy Sorrow there whilst mine alone
Are swoln too high t' admit of Lookers on.
[Ex. King weeping.

Philip returns weeping.

PHILIP - His Soul is fled to all Eternity;
And yet methought it did inform his Body,
That I, his darling Philip, was arriv'd
With Conquest on my Sword; and even in Death
Sent me his Joy in Smiles.

QUEEN ISABELLA - If Souls can after Death have any Sense
Of human things, his will be proud to know
That Philip is a Conqueror.

Enter Abdelazer.

But do not drown thy Laurels thus in Tears,
Such Tributes leave to us, thou art a Soldier.

PHILIP - Gods! this shou'd be my Mother

MENDOZO - It is, great Sir, the Queen.

PHILIP - Oh, she's too foul for one or t'other Title.

QUEEN ISABELLA - How, Sir, do you not know me?

PHILIP - When you were just, I did,
And with a Reverence, such as we pay Heav'n,
I paid my awful Duty;
But as you have abus'd my Royal Father,

For such a Sin the basest of your Slaves
Wou'd blush to call you Mother.

QUEEN ISABELLA - What means my Son?

PHILIP - Son! by Heav'n, I scorn the Title.

QUEEN ISABELLA - Oh Insolence! out of my sight, rude Boy.

PHILIP - We must not part so, Madam;
I first must let you know your Sin and Shame;
Nay, hear me calmly for, by Heav'n, you shall
My Father whilst he liv'd, tir'd his strong Arm
With numerous Battles 'gainst the Enemy,
Wasting his Brains in warlike Stratagems;
To bring Confusion on the faithless Moors,
Whilst you, lull'd in soft Peace at home, betray'd
His Name to everlasting Infamy;
Suffer'd his Bed to be defil'd with Lust,
Gave up your self, your Honour, and your Vows,
To wanton in yon sooty Lecher's Arms.
[Points to Abd.

ABDELAZER - Me, dost thou mean?

PHILIP - Yes, Villain, thee, thou Hell-begotten Fiend,
'Tis thee I mean.

QUEEN ISABELLA - Oh most unnatural, to dishonour me!

PHILIP - That Dog you mean, that has dishonour'd you,
Dishonour'd me, these Lords, nay, and all Spain;
This Devil's he, that

ABDELAZER - That, what. Oh pardon me if I throw off
All Ties of Duty: wert thou ten King's Sons,
And I as many Souls as I have Sins,
Thus I would hazard all.
[Draws, they all run between.

PHILIP - Stand off or I'll make way upon thy Bosom.

ABDELAZER - How got you, Sir, this daring?

PHILIP - From injur'd Philip's Death,
Who, whilst he liv'd, unjustly cherish'd thee,
And set thee up beyond the reach of Fate;
Blind with thy brutal Valor, deaf with thy Flatteries,
Discover'd not the Treason thou didst act,
Nor none durst let him know 'em but did he live,
I wou'd aloud proclaim them in his Ears.

ABDELAZER - You durst as well been damn'd.

PHILIP - Hell seize me if I want Revenge for this
Not dare!
Arise, thou injur'd Ghost of my dead King,
And thro thy dreadful Paleness dart a Horror,
May fright this pair of Vipers from their Sins.

ABDELAZER - Oh insupportable! dost hear me, Boy?

QUEEN ISABELLA - Are ye all mute, and hear me thus upbraided?
[To the Lords.

PHILIP - Dare ye detain me whilst the Traitor braves me?

MENDOZO - Forbear, my Prince, keep in that noble Heat
That shou'd be better us'd than on a Slave.

ABDELAZER - You politick Cheat

MENDOZO - Abdelazer
By the Authority of my Government,
Which yet I hold over the King of Spain,
By Warrant of a Council from the Peers,
And (as an Unbeliever) from the Church,
I utterly deprive thee of that Greatness,
Those Offices and Trusts you hold in Spain.

ABDELAZER - Cardinal, who lent thee this Commission?
Grandees of Spain, do you consent to this?

ALL - We do.

ALONZO - What Reason for it? let his Faith be try'd.

MENDOZO - It needs no tryal, the Proofs are evident,
And his Religion was his Veil for Treason.

ALONZO - Why should you question his Religion, Sir?
He does profess Christianity.

MENDOZO - Yes, witness his Habit which he still retains
In scorn to ours -
His Principles are too as unalterable.

ABDELAZER - Is that the only Argument you bring?
I tell thee, Cardinal, not thy Holy Gown
Covers a Soul more sanctify'd than this
Moorish Robe.

PHILIP - Damn his Religion, he has a thousand Crimes
That will yet better justify your Sentence.

MENDOZO - Come not within the Court; for if you do,
Worse mischief shall ensue you have your Sentence.
[Ex. Phil, and Men.

ALONZO - My Brother banish'd! 'tis very sudden;
For thy sake, Sister, this must be recall'd. [To Flor.

QUEEN ISABELLA - Alonzo, join with me, I'll to the King,
And check the Pride of this insulting Cardinal.
[Exeunt all, except Abdelazer, Florella.

ABDELAZER - Banish'd! if I digest this Gall,
May Cowards pluck the Wreath from off my Brow,
Which I have purchas'd with so many Wounds,
And all for Spain; for Spain! ingrateful Spain!
Oh, my Florella, all my Glory's vanish'd,
The Cardinal (Oh damn him) wou'd have me banish'd.

FLORELLA - But, Sir, I hope you will not tamely go.

ABDELAZER - Tamely! ha, ha, ha, yes, by all means
A very honest and religious Cardinal!

FLORELLA - I wou'd not for the World you should be banish'd.

ABDELAZER - Not Spain, you mean, for then she leaves the King. [Aside.
What if I be? Fools! not to know. All parts o' th' World
Allow enough for Villany; for I'll be brave no more.
It is a Crime and then I can live any where
But say I go from hence, I leave behind me
A Cardinal that will laugh. I leave behind me
A Philip that will clap his Hands in sport
But the worst Wound is this, I leave my Wrongs,
Dishonours, and my Discontents, all unreveng'd
Leave me, Florella, prithee do not weep;
I love thee, love thee wondrously, go leave me
I am not now at leisure to be fond
Go to your Chamber, go.

FLORELLA - No, to the King I'll fly,
And beg him to revenge thy Infamy. [Ex. Florella.
To him Alonzo.

ALONZO - The Cardinal's mad to have thee banish'd Spain.
I've left the Queen in angry Contradiction,
But yet I fear the Cardinal's Reasoning.

ABDELAZER - This Prince's Hate proceeds from Love,

He's jealous of the Queen, and fears my Power.   [Aside.

ALONZO - Come, rouse thy wonted Spirits, awake thy Soul,
And arm thy Justice with a brave Revenge.

ABDELAZER - I'll arm no Justice with a brave Revenge.
[Sullenly.

ALONZO - Shall they then triumph o'er thee, who were once
Proud to attend thy conqu'ring Chariot-Wheels?

ABDELAZER - I care not. I am a Dog, and can bear wrongs.

ALONZO - But, Sir, my Honour is concern'd with yours,
Since my lov'd Sister did become your Wife;
And if yours suffer, mine too is unsafe.

ABDELAZER - I cannot help it.

ALONZO - What Ice has chill'd thy Blood?
This Patience was not wont to dwell with thee.

ABDELAZER - 'Tis true; but now the World is chang'd you see.
Thou art too brave to know what I resolve   [Aside.
No more, here comes the King with my Florella.
He loves her, and she swears to me she's chaste;
'Tis well, if true, well too, if it be false: [Aside.
I care not, 'tis Revenge
That I must sacrifice my Love and Pleasure to.
[Alon. and Abd. stand aside.

Enter King, Lords, Guards passing over the Stage,
Florella in a suppliant posture weeping.

KING FERDINAND - Thou woo'st me to reverse thy Husband's Doom,
And I woo thee for Mercy on my self,
Why shoud'st thou sue to him for Life and Liberty,
For any other, who himself lies dying,
Imploring from thy Eyes a little Pity?

FLORELLA - Oh mighty King! in whose sole Power, like Heav'n,
The Lives and Safeties of your Slaves remain,
Hear and redress my Abdelazer's Wrongs.

KING FERDINAND - All Lives and Safeties in my Power remain!
Mistaken charming Creature, if my Power
Be such, who kneel and bow to thee,
What must thine be,
Who hast the Sovereign Command o'er me and it?
Wou'dst thou give Life? turn but thy lovely Eyes
Upon the wretched thing that wants it,

And he will surely live, and live for ever.
Canst thou do this, and com'st to beg of me?

FLORELLA - Alas, Sir, what I beg's what you alone can give,
My Abdelazer's Pardon.

KING FERDINAND - Pardon! can any thing ally'd to thee offend?
Thou art so sacred and so innocent,
That but to know thee, and to look on thee,
Must change even Vice to Virtue.
Oh my Florella!
So perfectly thou dost possess my Soul,
That ev'ry Wish of thine shall be obey'd:
Say, wou'dst thou have thy Husband share my Crown?
Do but submit to love me, and I yield it.

FLORELLA - Such Love as humble Subjects owe their King.
[Kneels, he takes her up.
And such as I dare pay, I offer here.

KING FERDINAND - I must confess it is a Price too glorious:
But, my Florella -

ABDELAZER - I'll interrupt your amorous Discourse. [Aside.
[Abdelazer comes up to them.

FLORELLA - Sir, Abdelazer's here.

KING FERDINAND - His Presence never was less welcome to me;
[Aside.
But, Madam, durst the Cardinal use this Insolence?
Where is your noble Husband?

ABDELAZER - He sees me, yet inquires for me. [Aside.

FLORELLA - Sir, my Lord is here.

KING FERDINAND - Abdelazer, I have heard with much surprize,
O' th' Injuries you've receiv'd, and mean to right you:
My Father lov'd you well, made you his General,
I think you worthy of that Honour still.

ABDELAZER - True, for my Wife's sake. [Aside.

KING FERDINAND - When my Coronation is solemnized,
Be present there, and re-assume your wonted State and Place;
And see how I will check the insolent Cardinal.

ABDELAZER - I humbly thank my Sovereign -
[Kneels, and kisses the King's Hand.
That he loves my Wife so well. [Aside.

[Exeunt.
Manent Abdelazer, Florella.

FLORELLA - Wilt thou not pay my Service with one Smile?
Have I not acted well the Suppliant's part?

ABDELAZER - Oh wonderfully! y'ave learnt the Art to move.
Go, leave me.

FLORELLA - Still out of humour, thoughtful and displeas'd?
And why at me, my Abdelazer? what have I done?

ABDELAZER - Rarely! you cannot do amiss you are so beautiful.
So very fair. Go, get you in, I say
[Turns her in roughly.
She has the art of dallying with my Soul,
Teaching it lazy softness from her Looks.
But now a nobler Passion's enter'd there,
And blows it thus to Air. Idol Ambition,
Florella must to thee a Victim fall:
Revenge, to thee a Cardinal and Prince:
And to my Love and Jealousy, a King
More yet, my mighty Deities, I'll do,
None that you e'er inspir'd like me shall act;
That fawning servile Crew shall follow next,
Who with the Cardinal cry'd, banish Abdelazer.

Like Eastern Monarchs I'll adorn thy Fate,
And to the Shades thou shalt descend in State.

[Exit.

ACT II.

SCENE I. A Chamber of State.

Enter the King crown'd, Philip, Mendozo, Queen, Leonora, Florella, Elvira, Alonzo, Roderigo, Ordonio, Sebastian, Antonio, Officers and Guards; met by Abdelazer follow'd by Osmin, Zarrack, and Moors attending. He comes in with Pride, staring on Philip and Mendozo, and takes his stand next the King.

PHILIP - Why stares the Devil thus, as if he meant
From his infectious Eyes to scatter Plagues,
And poison all the World? Was he not banish'd?
How dares the Traitor venture into th' Presence?
Guards, spurn the Villain forth.

ABDELAZER - Who spurns the Moor
Were better set his foot upon the Devil
Do, spurn me, and this Hand thus justly arm'd,

Shall like a Thunder-bolt, breaking the Clouds,
Divide his Body from his Soul, stand back -
[To the Guards.
Spurn Abdelazer!

PHILIP - Death, shall we bear this Insolence?

ALONZO - Great Sir, I think his Sentence was unjust.
[To the King.

MENDOZO - Sir, you're too partial to be judge in this,
And shall not give your Voice.

ABDELAZER - Proud Cardinal but he shall and give it loud.
And shall not! who shall hinder him?

PHILIP - This and cut his Wind-pipe too.
[Offers to draw.
To spoil his whisp'ring.
[Abd. offers to draw, his Attendants do the same.

KING FERDINAND - What means this Violence?
Forbear to draw your Swords, 'tis we command.

ABDELAZER - Sir, do me Justice, I demand no more.
[Kneels, and offers his Sword.
And at your Feet we lay our Weapons down.

MENDOZO - Sir, Abdelazer has had Justice done,
And stands by me banish'd the Court of Spain.

KING FERDINAND - How, Prince Cardinal!
From whence do you derive Authority
To banish him the Court without our leave?

MENDOZO - Sir, from my Care unto your royal Person,
As I'm your Governor then for the Kingdom's Safety.

KING FERDINAND - Because I was a Boy, must I be still so?
Time, Sir, has given me in that formal Ceremony,
And I am of an age to rule alone;
And from henceforth discharge you of your Care.
We know your near relation to this Crown,
And wanting Heirs, that you must fill the Throne;
Till when, Sir, I am absolute Monarch here,
And you must learn Obedience.

MENDOZO - Pardon my zealous Duty, which I hope
You will approve, and not recal his Banishment.

KING FERDINAND - Sir, but I will; and who dares contradict

It, is a Traitor.

PHILIP - I dare the first, yet do defy the last.

KING FERDINAND - My hot-brain'd Sir, I'll talk to you anon.

MENDOZO - Sir, I am wrong'd, and will appeal to Rome.

PHILIP - By Heav'n, I'll to the Camp, Brother, farewel,
When next I meet thee, it shall be in Arms,
If thou can'st get loose from thy Mistress' Chains,
Where thou ly'st drown'd in idle wanton Love.

ABDELAZER - Hah, his Mistress, who is't Prince Philip means?

PHILIP - Thy Wife, thy Wife, proud Moor, whom thou'rt content
To sell for Honour to eternal Infamy
Does't make thee snarl? Bite on, whilst thou shalt see,
I go for Vengeance, and 'twill come with me.
[Going out, turns and draws.

ABDELAZER - Stay! for 'tis here already, turn, proud Boy.
[Abdelazer draws.

KING FERDINAND - What mean you, Philip? [Talks to him aside.

QUEEN ISABELLA - Cease, cease your most impolitick Rage. [To Abdelazer.
Is this a time to shew't? Dear Son, you are a King,
And may allay this Tempest.

KING FERDINAND - How dare you disobey my Will and Pleasure? [To Abdelazer.

ABDELAZER - Shall I be calm, and hear my Wife call'd Whore?
Were he great Jove, and arm'd with all his Lightning,
By Heav'n, I could not hold my just Resentment.

QUEEN ISABELLA - 'Twas in his Passion, noble Abdelazer
[King talking to Phil. aside.
Imprudently thou dost disarm thy Rage,
And giv'st the Foe a warning, e'er thou strik'st;
When with thy Smiles thou might'st securely kill.
You know the Passion that the Cardinal bears me;
His Pow'r too o'er Philip, which well manag'd
Will serve to ruin both: put up your Sword
When next you draw it, teach it how to act.

ABDELAZER - You shame me, and command me.

QUEEN ISABELLA - Why all this Rage? does it become you, Sir?
[To Mendozo aside.
What is't you mean to do?

MENDOZO - You need not care, whilst Abdelazer's safe.

QUEEN ISABELLA - Jealousy, upon my Life, how gay it looks!

MENDOZO - Madam, you want that pitying Regard
To value what I do, or what I am;
I'll therefore lay my Cardinal's Hat aside,
And in bright Arms demand my Honour back.

QUEEN ISABELLA - Is't thus, my Lord, you give me Proofs of Love?
Have then my Eyes lost all their wonted Power?
And can you quit the hope of gaining me,
To follow your Revenge? go, go to fight,
Bear Arms against your Country, and your King,
All for a little worthless Honour lost.

MENDOZO - What is it, Madam, you would have me do?

QUEEN ISABELLA - Not side with Philip, as you hope my Grace
Now, Sir, you know my Pleasure, think on't well.

MENDOZO - Madam, you know your Power o'er your Slave,
And use it too tyrannically but dispose
The Fate of him, whose Honour, and whose Life,
Lies at your Mercy
I'll stay and die, since 'tis your gracious Pleasure.

KING FERDINAND - Philip, upon your Life,
Upon your strict Allegiance, I conjure you
To remain at Court, till I have reconcil'd you.

PHILIP - Never, Sir;
Nor can you bend my Temper to that Tameness.

KING FERDINAND - 'Tis in my Power to charge you as a Prisoner;
But you're my Brother, yet remember too
I am your King - No more.

PHILIP - I will obey.

KING FERDINAND - Abdelazer,
I beg you will forget your Cause of Hate
Against my Brother Philip, and the Cardinal;
He's young, and rash, but will be better temper'd.

ABDELAZER - Sir, I have done, and beg your royal Pardon.

KING FERDINAND - Come, Philip, give him your Hand.

PHILIP - I can forgive without a Ceremony.

KING FERDINAND - And to confirm ye Friends,
I invite you all to Night to banquet with me;
Pray see you give Attendance. Come, Brother,
You must along with us.

[Exeunt all but Abdelazer, Queen and Women.

QUEEN ISABELLA - Leave me
[To the Women, who go out.
Now my dear Moor.

ABDELAZER - Madam.

QUEEN ISABELLA - Why dost thou answer with that cold Reserve
Is that a Look, an Action for a Lover?

ABDELAZER - Ah, Madam

QUEEN ISABELLA - Have I not taken off thy Banishment?
Restor'd thee to thy former State and Honours?
Nay, and heap'd new ones too, too mighty for thy Hopes;
And still to raise thee equal to this Heart,
Where thou must ever reign.

ABDELAZER - 'Tis true, my bounteous Mistress, all this you've done
But -

QUEEN ISABELLA - But what, my Abdelazer?

ABDELAZER - I will not call it to your Memory.

QUEEN ISABELLA - What canst thou mean?

ABDELAZER - Why was the King remov'd?

QUEEN ISABELLA - To make thy way more easy to my Arms.

ABDELAZER - Was that all?

QUEEN ISABELLA - All!

ABDELAZER - Not but it is a Blessing Gods would languish for
But as you've made it free, so make it just.

QUEEN ISABELLA - Thou mean'st, marry thee.

ABDELAZER - No, by the Gods [Aside.
Not marry thee, unless I were a King.

QUEEN ISABELLA - What signifies the Name to him that rules one?

ABDELAZER - What use has he of Life, that cannot live
Without a Ruler?

QUEEN ISABELLA - Thou wouldst not have me kill him.

ABDELAZER - Oh, by no means, not for my wretched Life!
What, kill a King! forbid it, Heaven:
Angels stand like his Guards about his Person.
The King!
Not so many Worlds as there be Stars
Twinkling upon the embroider'd Firmament!
The King!
He loves my Wife Florella, shou'd he die
I know none else durst love her.

QUEEN ISABELLA - And that's the Reason you wou'd send him hence.

ABDELAZER - I must confess, I wou'd not bear a wrong:
But do not take me for a Villain, Madam;
He is my King, and may do what he pleases.

QUEEN ISABELLA - 'Tis well, Sir.

ABDELAZER - Again that Frown, it renders thee more charming
Than any other Dress thou could'st put on.

QUEEN ISABELLA - Away, you do not love me.

ABDELAZER - Now mayst thou hate me, if this be not pretty.

QUEEN ISABELLA - Oh, you can flatter finely

ABDELAZER - Not I, by Heaven:
Oh, that this Head were circled in a Crown,
And I were King, by Fortune, as by Birth!
And that I was, till by thy Husband's Power
I was divested in my Infancy
Then you shou'd see, I do not flatter ye.
But I, instead of that, must see my Crown
Bandy'd from Head to Head, and tamely see it:
And in this wretched state I live, 'tis true;
But with what Joy, you, if you lov'd, might guess.

QUEEN ISABELLA - We need no Crowns; Love best contented is
In shady Groves, and humble Cottages,
Where when 'twould sport, it safely may retreat,
Free from the Noise and Danger of the Great;
Where Victors are ambitious of no Bays,
But what their Nymphs bestow on Holy-days;
Nor Envy can the amorous Shepherd move,

Unless against a Rival in his Love.

ABDELAZER - Love and Ambition are the same to me,
In either I'll no Rivals brook.

QUEEN ISABELLA - Nor I:
And when the King you urge me to remove,
It may be from Ambition, not from Love.

ABDELAZER - Those Scruples did not in your Bosom dwell,
When you a King did in a Husband kill.

QUEEN ISABELLA - How, Sir, dare you upbraid me with that Sin,
To which your Perjuries first drew me in?

ABDELAZER - You interrupt my Sense; I only meant
A Sacrifice to Love so well begun
Shou'd not Devotion want to finish it;
And if that stop to all our Joys were gone,
The envying World wou'd to our Power submit:
But Kings are sacred, and the Gods alone
Their Crimes must judge, and punish too, or none
Yet he alone destroys his Happiness.

QUEEN ISABELLA - There's yet one more

ABDELAZER - One more! give me his Name,
And I will turn it to a Magick Spell,
To bind him ever fast.

QUEEN ISABELLA - Florella.

ABDELAZER - Florella! Oh, I cou'd gnaw my Chains
That humble me so low as to adore her: [Aside.
But the fond Blaze must out while I erect
A nobler Fire more fit for my Ambition.
Florella dies, a Victim to your Will.
I will not let you lose one single Wish,
For a poor Life, or two;
Tho I must see my Glories made a Prey,
And not demand 'em from the Ravisher;
Nor yet complain because he is my King:
But Philip's Brow no sacred Ointment deifies,
If he do wrong, stands fair for the Revenger.

QUEEN ISABELLA - Philip! instruct me how t' undo that Boy I hate;
The publick Infamy I have receiv'd,
I will revenge with nothing less than Death.

ABDELAZER - 'Tis well we can agree in our Resentments,
For I have vow'd he shall not live a day;

He has an Art to pry into our Secrets:
To all besides our Love is either hid,
Or else they dare not see. But this Prince
Has a most dangerous Spirit must be calm'd.

QUEEN ISABELLA - I have resolv'd his Death,
And now have waiting in my Cabinet,
Engines to carry on this mighty Work of my Revenge.

ABDELAZER - Leave that to me, who equally am injur'd;
You, like the Gods, need only but command,
And I will execute your sacred Will
That done, there's none dare whisper what we do.

QUEEN ISABELLA - Nature, be gone, I chase thee from my Soul,
Who Love's almighty Empire does controul:
And she that will to thy dull Laws submit,
In spite of thee, betrays the Hypocrite.
No rigid Virtue shall my Soul possess,
Let Gown-men preach against the Wickedness;
Pleasures were made by Gods, and meant for us,
And not t' enjoy 'em, were ridiculous.

ABDELAZER - Oh perfect, great and glorious of thy Sex!
Like thy great self 'twas spoke, resolv'd and brave
I must attend the King, where I will watch
All Philip's Motions.

QUEEN ISABELLA - And, after that, if you will beg Admittance,
I'll give you leave to visit me to Night.

ABDELAZER - Madam, that Blessing now must be defer'd.
[Leads her to the Door.
My Wrongs and I will be retir'd to Night,
And bring forth Vengeance with the Morning's Light.

Enter Osmin, Zarrack.

OSMIN - My gracious Lord.

ABDELAZER - Come near and take a Secret from my Lips;
And he who keeps not silent hears his Death.
This Night the Prince and Cardinal, do you mark me
Are murder'd.

OSMIN - Where, Sir?

ABDELAZER - Here in the Court.

OSMIN - By whom, great Sir?

ABDELAZER - By thee, I know thou darst.

OSMIN - Whatever you command.

ABDELAZER - Good! then see it be perform'd.
Osmin, how goes the Night?

OSMIN - About the hour of Eight,
And you're expected at the Banquet, Sir:
Prince Philip storms, and swears you're with the Queen.

ABDELAZER - Let him storm on; the Tempest will be laid
Where's my Wife?

OSMIN - In the Presence, Sir, with the Princess and
Other Ladies.

ABDELAZER - She's wondrous forward! what the King
(I am not jealous tho) but he makes court to her.
Hah, Osmin!
He throws out Love from Eyes all languishing;
Come tell me, he does sigh to her, no matter if he do
And fawns upon her Hand, and kneels; tell me, Slave!

OSMIN - Sir, I saw nothing like to Love; he only treats her
Equal to her Quality.

ABDELAZER - Oh, damn her Quality.

ZARRACK - I came just now
From waiting on his Person to the Banquet,
And heard him ask, if he might visit her to Night,
Having something to impart to her, that concern'd his Life.

ABDELAZER - And so it shall, by Heav'n! [Aside.

ZARRACK - But she deny'd, and he the more intreated
But all in vain, Sir.

ABDELAZER - Go, Osmin, (you the Captain of my Guard of Moors)
Chuse out the best affected Officers,
To keep the Watch to Night
Let every Guard be doubled, you may be liberal too
And when I gave the Word, be ready all.

OSMIN - What shall the Word be?
[Ex. Zarrack.

ABDELAZER - Why - Treason, mean time make it your Business,
To watch the Prince's coming from the Banquet;
Heated with Wine, and fearless of his Person,

You'll find him easily to be attack'd.

OSMIN - Sir, do not doubt my Management nor Success.
[Ex. Osmin.

ABDELAZER - So, I thank thee, Nature, that in making me,
Thou didst design me Villain;
Hitting each Faculty for active Mischief:
Thou skilful Artist, thank thee for my Face,
It will discover nought that's hid within.
Thus arm'd for Ills,
Darkness, and Horrour, I invoke your aid;
And thou dread Night, shade all your busy Stars
In blackest Clouds,
And let my Dagger's Brightness only serve
To guide me to the Mark and guide it so,
It may undo a Kingdom at one Blow.

[Exit.

SCENE II. A Banqueting Hall.

A Banquet, under a Canopy the King, Leonora, Florella, Ladies waiting; Philip, Mendozo, Alonzo, Ordonio, Antonio, Sebastian, Lords and Attendants: As soon as the Scene draws off, they all rise, and come forward.

KING FERDINAND - My Lords, you're sad to Night; give us loud Musick -
I have a double Cause to mourn;
And Grief has taken up his dwelling here
Beyond the Art of Love, or Wine to conquer
'Tis true, my Father's dead and possibly
'Tis not so decent to appear thus gay;
But Life, and Death, are equal to the wretched,
And whilst Florella frowns, 'tis in that Number [To Florella
I must account her Slave, Alonzo,
How came thy Father so bewitch'd to Valour,
(For Abdelazer has no other Virtue)
To recompense it with so fair a Creature?
Was this a Treasure t' inrich the Devil with?

ALONZO - Sir, he has many Virtues, more than Courage,
Royally born, serv'd well his King, and Country;
My Father brought him up to martial Toils,
And taught him to be brave; I hope, and good;
Beside, he was your Royal Father's Favourite.

KING FERDINAND - No, Alonzo, 'twas not his Love to Virtue,
But nice Obedience to his King, and Master,
Who seeing my increase of Passion for her,
To kill my Hopes, he gave her to this Moor.

ALONZO - She's now a virtuous Woman, Sir.

KING FERDINAND - Politick Sir, who would have made her other?
Against her Will, he forc'd her to his Arms,
Whilst all the World was wondring at his Madness.

ALONZO - He did it with her Approbation, Sir.

KING FERDINAND - With thine, Florella! cou'dst thou be so criminal?

FLORELLA - Sir, I was ever taught Obedience;
My humble Thoughts durst ne'er aspire to you,
And next to that - Death, or the Moor, or any thing.

KING FERDINAND - Oh God! had I then told my Tale
So feebly, it could not gain Belief.
Oh my Florella! this little Faith of thine
Has quite undone thy King, Alonzo,
Why didst not thou forbid this fatal Marriage,
She being thy only Sister?

ALONZO - Great Sir, I did oppose it with what Violence
My Duty would permit; and wou'd have dy'd
In a just Quarrel of her dear Defence;
And, Sir, though I submitted to my Father,
The Moor and I stand on unequal Terms.

PHILIP - Come, who dares drink Confusion to this Moor?

ANTONIO - That, Sir, will I.

SEBASTIAN - And I.

PHILIP - Page, fill my Glass, I will begin the Round,
Ye all shall pledge it, Alonzo, first to thee.
[Drinks.

ALONZO - To me, Sir!

PHILIP - Why, yes, thou lovest him, therefore
Nay, you shall drink it, tho 'twere o'th' Stygian Lake.
Take it, by Heaven, thoud'st pimp for him to my Mother
Nay, and after that, give him another Sister.

ALONZO - 'Tis well you are my Prince.

PHILIP - I'd rather be a Prince of Curs, come pledge me

ALONZO - Well, Sir, I'll give you way.
[Drinks.

PHILIP - So wou'dst thou any, though they trod on thee.
So, nay, Prince Cardinal, tho it be not decent
For one so sanctify'd to drink a Health;
Yet 'tis your Office both to damn and bless
Come, drink and damn the Moor.

MENDOZO - Sir, I'm for no carousing.

PHILIP - I'm in an Humour now to be obey'd,
And must not be deny'd. But see, the Moor
Enter Abdelazer, gazes on them.
Just come to pledge at last. Page, fill again.

ABDELAZER - I'll do you Reason, Prince, what'er it be.
[Gives him the Glass.

PHILIP - 'Twas kindly said. Confusion to the Moor.

ABDELAZER - Confusion to the Moor, if this vain Boy,
See the next rising Sun. [Aside.

PHILIP - Well done, my Lad.

KING FERDINAND - Abdelazer, you have been missing long,
The publick Good takes up your whole Concern,
But we shall shortly ease you of that Load
Come, let's have some Musick;
Ordonio, did I not call for Musick?

ORDONIO - You did, Sir.

ABDELAZER - Roderigo!

RODERIGO - My gracious Lord
[Roderigo whispers to Abdelazer.

ABDELAZER - No more, the Prince observes us.

PHILIP - There's no good towards when you are whisp'ring.

ORDONIO - The Musick you commanded, Sir, is ready.

SONG.

Nymph.

Make haste, Amintas, come away,
The Sun is up and will not stay;
And oh how very short's a Lover's Day!
Make haste, Amintas, to this Grove,

Beneath whose Shade so oft I've sat,
And heard my dear lay'd Swain repeat,
How much he Galatea lov'd;
Whilst all the listening Birds around,
Sung to the Musick of the blessed Sound.

Make haste, Amintas, come away,
The Sun is up and will not stay;
And oh how very short's a Lover's Day!

Swain enters, with Shepherds and Shepherdesses, and Pipes.

I hear thy charming Voice, my Fair,
And see, bright Nymph, thy Swain is here;
Who his Devotions had much earlier paid,
But that a Lamb of thine was stray'd;
And I the little Wanderer have brought,
That with one angry Look from thy fair Eyes,
Thou may'st the little Fugitive chastise,
Too great a Punishment for any Fault.
Come, Galatea, haste away,
The Sun is up and will not stay,
And oh how very short's a Lover's Day! [Dance.

KING FERDINAND - How likes Florella this?

FLORELLA - Sir, all Delight's so banish'd from my Soul,
I've lost the Taste of every single Joy.

ABDELAZER - God's! this is fine! Give me your Art of Flattery,
Or something more of this, will ruin me
Tho I've resolv'd her Death, yet whilst she's mine,
I would not have her blown by Summer Flies.

PHILIP - Mark how he snarls upon the King!
The Cur will bite anon.

ABDELAZER - Come, my Florella, is't not Bed-time, Love?

FLORELLA - I'll wait upon you, Sir.
[Going out.

PHILIP - The Moor has ta'en away, we may depart.

ABDELAZER - What has he ta'en away?
[Turns about.

PHILIP - The fine gay play-thing, that made us all so merry.

ABDELAZER - Was this your Sport? [To his Wife.

KING FERDINAND - Abdelazer, keep your way. Good night, fair Creature!

ABDELAZER - I will obey for once.

[Ex. Abdelazer and Florella.

KING FERDINAND - Why this Resentment, Brother, and in publick?

PHILIP - Because he gives me Cause, and that in Publick.
And, Sir, I was not born to bear with Insolence;
I saw him dart Revenge from both his Eyes,
And bite his angry Lip between his Teeth,
To keep his Jealousy from breaking forth,
Which, when it does, stand fast, my King.

KING FERDINAND - But, Philip, we will find a way to check him;
Till when we must dissemble, take my Counsel. Good night.

PHILIP - I cannot, nor I will not, yet good Night.
[Exit King, and all but Philip's Party.
Well, Friends, I see the King will sleep away his Anger,
And tamely see us murder'd by this Moor;
But I'll be active, Boys
Therefore, Antonio, you command the Horse;
Get what more Numbers to our Cause you can:
'Tis a good Cause, and will advance our Credit.
We will awake this King out of his Lethargy of Love,
And make him absolute. Go to your Charge,
And early in the Morning I'll be with you
[Ex. all but Phil.
If all fail, Portugal shall be my Refuge,
Those whom so late I conquer'd, shall protect me
But this Alanzo I shou'd make an Interest in;
Cou'd I but flatter, 'tis a Youth that's brave.

Enter Cardinal in haste.

MENDOZO - Fly, fly, my Prince, we are betray'd and lost else.

PHILIP - Betray'd and lost! Dreams, idle Coward Dreams.

MENDOZO - Sir, by my Holy Order, I'm in earnest,
And you must either quickly fly, or die;
'Tis so ordain'd, nor have I time to tell
By what strange Miracle I learn'd our Fate.

PHILIP - Nor care I, I will stay, and brave it.

MENDOZO - That, Sir, you shall not, there's no safety here,
And 'tis the Army only can secure us.

PHILIP - Where had you this Intelligence?

MENDOZO - I'll tell you as we go to my Apartment;
Where we must put ourselves in Holy Dress;
For so the Guards are set in every Place,
(And those all Moors, the Slaves of Abdelazer)
That 'tis impossible in any other Habit to escape.
Come, haste with me, and let us put 'em on.

PHILIP - I had rather stay and kill till I am weary
Let's to the Queen's Apartment and seize this Moor;
I'm sure there the Mongrel's kennel'd.

MENDOZO - Sir, we lose time in talking. Come with me.

PHILIP - Where be these lousy Gaberdines?

MENDOZO - I will conduct you to 'em.

PHILIP - Mother and Moor, farewel,
I'll visit you again; and if I do,
My black Infernal, I will conjure you.

[Exeunt.

ACT III.

SCENE I. A Gallery in the Palace.

Enter Abdelazer and Zarrack.

ZARRACK - Osmin (my Lord) by this has done his Task,
And Philip is no more among the living:
Will you not rest to night?

ABDELAZER - Is this a time for Sleep and Idleness, dull Slaves?

ZARRACK - The Bus'ness we have Order, Sir, to do,
We can without your Aid.

Enter Osmin.

ABDELAZER - Osmin!
Thy ominous Looks presage an ill Success;
Thy Eyes no joyful News of Murders tell:
I thought I shou'd have seen thee drest in Blood
Speak! Speak thy News
Say that he lives, and let it be thy last.

OSMIN - Yes, Sir, he lives.

ABDELAZER - Lives! thou ly'st, base Coward lives! renounce thy Gods!
It were a Sin less dangerous - speak again.

OSMIN - Sir, Philip lives.

ABDELAZER - Oh treacherous Slave!

OSMIN - Not by my Fault, by Heav'n!

ABDELAZER - By what curst Chance,
If not from thee, could he evade his Fate?

OSMIN - By some Intelligence from his good Angel.

ABDELAZER - From his good Devil!
Gods! must the Earth another Day at once
Bear him and me alive?

OSMIN - Another Day! an Age for ought I know;
For, Sir, the Prince is fled, the Cardinal too.

ABDELAZER - Fled! fled, say'st thou?
Oh, I cou'd curse the Stars, that rule this Night:
'Tis to the Camp they're fled; the only Refuge
That Gods, or Men cou'd give 'em
Where got you this Intelligence?

OSMIN - My Lord, inquiring for the Prince
At the Apartment of the Cardinal, (whither he went)
His Pages answer'd me, he was at his Devotions:
A lucky time (I thought) to do the Deed;
And breaking in, found only their empty Habits,
And a poor sleepy Groom, who with much threatning,
Confess'd that they were fled, in holy Robes.

ABDELAZER - That Case of Sanctity was first ordain'd,
To cheat the honest World:
Twas an unlucky Chance but we are idle
Let's see, how from this ill, we may advance a good
[Pauses.
'Tis now dead time of Night, when Rapes, and Murders
Are hid beneath the horrid Veil of Darkness
I'll ring thro all the Court, with doleful Sound
The sad Alarms of Murder. Murder, Zarrack,
Take up thy standing yonder, Osmin, thou
At the Queen's Apartment, cry out, Murder:
Whilst I, like his ill Genius, do awake the King;
Perhaps in this Disorder I may kill him. [Aside.
Treason - Murder - Murder - Treason.

Enter Alonzo, and Courtiers.

ALONZO - What dismal Crys are these?

ABDELAZER - Where is the King? Treason. Murder!
Where is the sleeping Queen? Arise, arise.

OSMIN - The Devil taught him all his Arts of Falshood. [Aside.

Enter King in a Night-Gown, with Lights.

KING FERDINAND - Who frights our quiet Slumbers with this Noise?

Enter Queen Isabella and Women, with Lights.

QUEEN ISABELLA - Was it a Dream, or did I hear the Sound
Of Treason, call me from my silent Griefs?

KING FERDINAND - Who rais'd this Rumour, Abdelazer, you?

ABDELAZER - I did, Great Sir.

KING FERDINAND - Your Reasons.

ABDELAZER - Oh Sir, your Brother Philip, and the Cardinal,
Both animated by a Sense of Wrongs,
(And envying, Sir, the Fortune of your Slave)
Had laid a Plot this Night, to murder you:
And 'cause they knew it was my waiting Night,
They wou'd have laid the Treason, Sir, on me.

KING FERDINAND - The Cardinal, and my Brother! bring them forth,
Their Lives shall answer it.

ABDELAZER - Sir, 'tis impossible:
For when they found their Villany discover'd,
They in two Friers Habits made escape.

KING FERDINAND - That Cardinal is subtle, and ambitious,
And from him Philip learnt his dangerous Principles.

QUEEN ISABELLA - The Ambition of the one infects the other,
And they are both too dangerous to live
But might a Mother's Counsel be obey'd,
I wou'd advise you, send the valiant Moor
To fetch 'em back, e'er they can reach the Camp:
For thither they are fled where they will find
A Welcome fatal to us all.

KING FERDINAND - Madam, you counsel well; and, Abdelazer,

Make it your Care to fetch these Traitors back,
Not only for my Safety, and the Kingdom's,
But as they are your Enemies; and th' envious World
Will say, you made this story to undo 'em.

ABDELAZER - Sir, I'll obey; nor will I know repose,
Till I have justify'd this fatal Truth.
[Abdelazer goes to the Queen, and talks to her.

KING FERDINAND - Mean time I will to my Florella's Lodging,
Silence, and Night, are the best Advocates [Aside.
To plead a Lover's Cause. Abdelazer, haste.
Madam, I'll wait on you to your Chamber.

ABDELAZER - Sir, that's my Duty.

KING FERDINAND - Madam, good Night. Alonzo, to your rest.
[Ex. all but Queen Isabella and Abdelazer.

QUEEN ISABELLA - Philip escap'd!
Oh, that I were upon some Desart Shoar,
Where I might only to the Waves and Winds
Breathe out my Sense of Rage for this Defeat.

ABDELAZER - Oh, 'tis no time for Rage, but Action, Madam.

QUEEN ISABELLA - Give me but any Hopes of blest Revenge,
And I will be as calm as happy Lovers.

ABDELAZER - There is a way, and is but that alone;
But such a way, as never must be nam'd.

QUEEN ISABELLA - How! not be nam'd! Oh, swear thou hat'st me rather,
It were a Torment equal to thy Silence.

ABDELAZER - I'll shew my Passion rather in that Silence.

QUEEN ISABELLA - Kind Torturer, what mean'st thou?

ABDELAZER - To shew you, Madam, I had rather live
Wrong'd and contemn'd by Philip,
Than have your dearer Name made infamous.

QUEEN ISABELLA - Heavens! dost thou mock my Rage? can any Sin
I could commit, undo my Honour more
Than his late Insolence?
Oh, name me something may revenge that Shame:
I wou'd encounter killing Plagues, or Fire,
To meet it. Come, oh quickly give me ease.

ABDELAZER - I dare no more reveal the guilty Secret,

Than you dare execute it when 'tis told.

QUEEN ISABELLA - How little I am understood by thee
Come, tell me instantly, for I grow impatient;
You shall obey me, nay, I do command you.

ABDELAZER - Durst you proclaim. Philip a Bastard, Madam?

QUEEN ISABELLA - Hah! proclaim my self
What he wou'd have me thought!
What mean'st thou?

ABDELAZER - Instruct you in the way to your Revenge.

QUEEN ISABELLA - Upon my self thou meanest

ABDELAZER - No
He's now fled to th' Camp, where he'll be fortify'd
Beyond our Power to hurt, but by this means;
Which takes away his Hopes of being a King,
(For he'd no other Aim in taking Arms)
And leaves him open to the People's Scorn;
Whom own'd as King, Numbers wou'd assist him,
And then our Lives he may dispose,
As he has done our Honours.

QUEEN ISABELLA - There's Reason in thy Words: but oh my Fame!

ABDELAZER - Which I, by Heaven, am much more tender of,
Than my own Life or Honour; and I've a way
To save that too, which I'll at leisure tell you.
In the mean time send for your Confessor,
And with a borrow'd Penitence confess,
Their Idol Philip is a Bastard;
And zealously pretend you're urg'd by Conscience,
A cheap Pretence to cozen Fools withal.

QUEEN ISABELLA - Revenge, although I court you with my fatal Ruin,
I must enjoy thee: there's no other way,
And I'm resolv'd upon the mighty Pleasure;
He has profan'd my purer Flame for thee,
And merits to partake the Infamy.
[He leads her out.

ABDELAZER - Now have at my young King
I know he means to cuckold me to Night,
Whilst he believes I'll tamely step aside
No, let Philip and the Cardinal gain the Camp,
I will not hinder 'em
I have a nobler Sacrifice to make
To my declining Honour, shall redeem it,

And pay it back with Interest, well, then in order to't,
I'll watch about the Lodgings of Florella,
And if I see this hot young Lover enter,
I'll save my Wife the trouble of allaying
The amorous Heat, this will more nimbly do't,
[Snatches out his Dagger.
And do it once for all

Enter Florella in her Night-Clothes.

FLORELLA - My Abdelazer, why in that fierce posture,
As if thy Thoughts were always bent on Death?
Why is that Dagger out? against whom drawn?

ABDELAZER - Or stay, suppose I let him see Florella,
And when he's high with the expected Bliss,
Then take him thus. Oh, 'twere a fine surprize!

FLORELLA - My Lord, dear Abdelazer.

ABDELAZER - Or say, I made her kill him, that were yet
An Action much more worthy of my Vengeance.

FLORELLA - Will you not speak to me? what have I done?

ABDELAZER - By Heaven, it shall be so.

FLORELLA - What shall be so?

ABDELAZER - Hah -

FLORELLA - Why dost thou dress thy Eyes in such unusual wonder?
There's nothing here that is a stranger to thee,
Or what is not intirely thine own.

ABDELAZER - Mine!

FLORELLA - Thou canst not doubt it.

ABDELAZER - No, and for a proof that thou art so, take this Dagger.

FLORELLA - Alas, Sir! what to do?

ABDELAZER - To stab a Heart, Florella, a Heart that loves thee.

FLORELLA - Heaven forbid!

ABDELAZER - No matter what Heaven will, I say it must

FLORELLA - What must?

ABDELAZER - That Dagger must enter the Heart of him
That loves thee best, Florella; guess the Man.

FLORELLA - What means my Moor?
Wouldst thou have me kill thy self?

ABDELAZER – Yes, when I love thee better than the King.

FLORELLA - Ah, Sir! what mean you?

ABDELAZER - To have you kill this King,
When next he does pursue thee with his Love
What, do you weep?
By Heaven, they shall be bloody Tears then.

FLORELLA - I shall deserve them when I suffer Love
That is not fit to hear; but for the King,
That which he pays me, is so innocent

ABDELAZER - So innocent! damn thy dissembling Tongue;
Did I not see, with what fierce wishing Eyes
He gazed upon thy Face, whilst yours as wantonly
Returned, and understood the amorous Language?

FLORELLA - Admit it true, that such his Passions were,
As (Heaven's my witness) I've no cause to fear;
Have not I Virtue to resist his Flame,
Without a pointed Steel?

ABDELAZER - Your Virtue! Curse on the weak Defence;
Your Virtue's equal to his Innocence.
Here, take this Dagger, and if this Night he visit thee,
When he least thinks on't, send it to his Heart.

FLORELLA - If you suspect me, do not leave me, Sir.

ABDELAZER - Oh, I'm dispatch'd away, to leave you free
About a wonderful Affair, mean time,
I know you will be visited but as you wish to live,
At my return let me behold him dead.
Be sure you do't, 'tis for thy Honour's safety
I love thee so, that I can take no rest,
Till thou hast kill'd thy Image in his Breast.
Adieu, my dear Florella.
[Exit.

FLORELLA - Murder my King! the Man that loves me too
What Fiend, what Fury such an act wou'd do?
My trembling Hand wou'd not the Weapon bear,
And I should sooner strike it here than there.
[Pointing to her Breast.

No! though of all I am, this Hand alone
Is what thou canst command, as being thy own;
Yet this has plighted no such cruel Vow;
No Duty binds me to obey thee 'now.
To save my King's, my Life I will expose,
No Martyr dies in a more glorious Cause.

[Exit.

SCENE II. The Queen's Apartments.

Enter the Queen in an undress alone, with a Light.

QUEEN ISABELLA - Thou grateful Night, to whom all happy Lovers
Make their devout and humble Invocations;
Thou Court of Silence, where the God of Love,
Lays by the awful Terror of a Deity,
And every harmful Dart, and deals around
His kind Desires; whilst thou, blest Friend to Joys,
Draw'st all thy Curtains, made of gloomy Shades,
To veil the Blushes of soft yielding Maids;
Beneath thy Covert grant the Love-sick King,
May find admittance to Florella's Arms;
And being there, keep back the busy Day;
Maintain thy Empire till my Moor returns;
Where in her Lodgings he shall find his Wife,
Amidst her amorous Dalliance with my Son.
My watchful Spies are waiting for the Knowledge;
Which when to me imparted, I'll improve,
Till my Revenge be equal to my Love.

Enter Elvira.

Elvira, in thy Looks I read Success;
What hast thou learnt?

ELVIRA - Madam, the King is gone as you imagin'd,
To fair Florella's Lodging.

QUEEN ISABELLA - But art thou sure he gain'd Admittance?

ELVIRA - Yes, Madam;
But what Welcome he has found, to me's unknown;
But I believe it must be great, and kind.

QUEEN ISABELLA - I am of thy Opinion.
But now, Elvira, for a well-laid Plot,
To ruin this Florella; though she be innocent,
Yet she must die; so hard a Destiny
My Passion for her Husband does decree:

But 'tis the way I stop at.
His Jealousy already I have rais'd;
That's not enough, his Honour must be touch'd.
This Meeting twixt the King and fair Florella,
Must then be render'd publick;
'Tis the Disgrace, not Action, must incense him
Go you to Don Alonzo's Lodging strait,
Whilst I prepare my Story for his Ear.
[Exit Elvira.
Assist me all that's ill in Woman-kind,
And furnish me with Sighs, and feigned Tears,
That may express a Grief for this Discovery.
My Son, be like thy Mother, hot and bold;
And like the noble Ravisher of Rome,
Court her with Daggers, when thy Tongue grows faint,
Till thou hast made a Conquest o'er her Virtue.
Enter Alonzo, Elvira.
Oh, Alonzo, I have strange News to tell thee!

ALONZO - It must be strange indeed, that makes my Queen
Dress her fair Eyes in Sorrow.

QUEEN ISABELLA - It is a Dress that thou wilt be in love with,
When thou shalt hear my Story.
You had a Sister once.

ALONZO - Had!

QUEEN ISABELLA - Yes, had, whilst she was like thy self, all Virtue;
Till her bewitching Eyes kindled such Flames,
As will undo us all.

ALONZO - My Sister, Madam! sure it cannot be:
What Eyes? what Flames? inform me strait.

QUEEN ALONZO - Alonzo, thou art honest, just and brave:
And should I tell thee more,
(Knowing thy Loyalty's above all Nature)
It would oblige thee to commit an Outrage,
Which baser Spirits will call Cruelty.

ALONZO - Gods, Madam! do not praise my Virtue thus,
Which is so poor, it scarce affords me patience
To attend the end of what you wou'd deliver
Come, Madam, say my Sister is a Whore.
I know 'tis so you mean; and being so,
Where shall I kneel for Justice?
Since he that shou'd afford it me,
Has made her Criminal.
Pardon me, Madam, 'tis the King I mean.

QUEEN ISABELLA - I grieve to own, all thy prophetick Fears
Are true, Alonzo, 'tis indeed the King.

ALONZO - Then I'm disarm'd,
For Heaven can only punish him.

QUEEN ISABELLA - But, Alonzo,
Whilst that religious Patience dwells about thee,
All Spain must suffer, nay, Ages that shall ensue
Shall curse thy Name, and Family;
From whom a Race of Bastards shall proceed,
To wear that Crown.

ALONZO - No, Madam, not for mine,
My Sister's in my power, her Honour's mine;
I can command her Life, though not my King's.
Her Mother is a Saint, and shou'd she now
Look down from Heaven upon a Deed so foul,
I think even there she wou'd invent a Curse,
To thunder on her Head.
But, Madam, whence was this Intelligence?

QUEEN ISABELLA - Elvira saw the King enter her Lodgings,
With Lover's haste, and Joy.

ALONZO - Her Lodgings! When?

QUEEN ISABELLA - Now, not an Hour ago,
Now, since the Moor departed.

ALONZO - Damnation on her! can she be thus false?
Come, lead me to the Lodgings of this Strumpet,
And make me see this truth, [To Elvira.
Or I will leave thee dead, for thus abusing me.

QUEEN ISABELLA - Nay, dear Alonzo, do not go inrag'd,
Stay till your Temper wears a calmer look;
That if, by chance, you shou'd behold the Wantons,
In little harmless Dalliance, such as Lovers
(Aided with Silence, and the shades of Night)
May possibly commit,
You may not do that which you may repent of.

ALONZO - Gods! should I play the Pander!
And with my Patience, aid the amorous Sin
No, I shall scarce have so much Tameness left,
To mind me of my Duty to my King.
Ye Gods! behold the Sacrifice I make
To my lost Honour: behold, and aid my Justice.
[Ex. Alonzo.

QUEEN ISABELLA - It will concern me too to see this Wonder,
For yet I scarce can credit it.

[Exeunt.

SCENE III. Florella's Lodgings.

Enter the King, leading in Florella all in fear.

FLORELLA - Ah, Sir, the Gods and you would be more merciful,
If by a Death less cruel than my Fears,
You would preserve my Honour; begin it quickly,
And after that I will retain my Duty,
And at your Feet breathe Thanks in dying Sighs.

KING FERDINAND - Where learnt you, Fairest, so much Cruelty
To charge me with the Power of injuring thee?
Not from my Eyes, where Love and Languishment
Too sensibly inform thee of my Heart.

FLORELLA - Call it not Injury, Sir, to free my Soul
From fears which such a Visit must create,
In dead of Night, when nought but frightful Ghosts
Of restless Souls departed walk the Round.

KING FERDINAND - That fleeting thing am I, whom all Repose,
All Joys, and every good of Life abandon'd,
That fatal Hour thou gavest thy self away;
And I was doom'd to endless Desperation:
Yet whilst I liv'd, all glorious with my hopes,
Some sacred Treasures in thy Breast I hid,
And near thee still my greedy Soul will hover.

FLORELLA - Ah, rather like a Ravisher you come,
With Love and Fierceness in your dangerous Eyes;
And both will equally be fatal to me.

KING FERDINAND - Oh, do not fear me, as the fair Lucretia
Did the fierce Roman Youth; I mean no Rapes,
Thou canst not think that I wou'd force those Joys,
Which cease to be so, when compell'd, Florella
No, I would sooner pierce this faithful Heart,
Whose Flame appears too criminal for your Mercy.

FLORELLA - Why do you fright me, Sir? methinks your Looks
All pale, your Eyes thus fixt, and trembling Hands,
The awful Horror of the dark and silent Night,
Strike a cold Terror round my fainting Heart,
That does presage some fatal Accident.

KING FERDINAND - 'Tis in your cruel Eyes the Danger lies
Wou'd you receive me with that usual Tenderness,
Which did express it self in every Smile,
I should dismiss tin's Horror from my Face,
And place again its native Calmness there;
And all my Veins shall re-assume their Heat,
And with a new and grateful Ardour beat.

FLORELLA - Sir, all my Soul is taken up with fear,
And you advance your Fate, by staying here
Fly, fly, this place of Death, if Abdelazer
Shou'd find you here all the Divinity
About your sacred Person could not guard you.

KING FERDINAND - Ah, my Florella, cease thy needless Fear,
And in thy Soul let nothing reign but Love;
Love, that with soft Desires may fill thy Eyes,
And save thy Tongue the pain t' instruct my Heart,
In the most grateful Knowledge Heaven can give me.

FLORELLA - That Knowledge, Sir, wou'd make us both more wretched,
Since you, I know, wou'd still be wishing on,
And I shou'd grant, till we were both undone.
And, Sir, how little she were worth your care,
Cou'd part with all her honourable Fame,
For an inglorious Life, short and despis'd

KING FERDINAND - Canst thou believe a Flame thy Eyes have kindled,
Can urge me to an infamous pursuit?
No, my Florella, I adore thy Virtue,
And none profane those Shrines, to whom they offer;
Say but thou lov'st and I thus low will bow
[Kneels.
And sue to thee, to be my Sovereign Queen?
I'll circle thy bright Forehead with the Crowns
Of Castile, Portugal, and Arragon;
And all those petty Kingdoms, which do bow
Their Tributary Knees to thy Adorer.

FLORELLA - Ah, Sir! have you forgot my sacred Vow?
All that I am, is Abdelazer's now.

KING FERDINAND - By Heav'n, it was a sacrilegious Theft;
But I the Treasure from his Breast will tear,
And reach his Heart, though thou art seated there.

FLORELLA - A Deed like that my Virtue wou'd undo,
And leave a Stain upon your Glories too;
A Sin, that wou'd my Hate, not Passion move;
I owe a Duty, where I cannot love.

KING FERDINAND - Thou think'st it then no Sin to kill thy King;
For I must die, without thy Love, Florella.

FLORELLA - How tamely, Sir, you with the Serpent play,
Whose fatal Poison must your Life betray;
And though a King, cannot divine your Fate;
Kings only differ from the Gods in that.
See, Sir, with this, I am your Murderer made;
[Holds up a Dagger.
By those we love, we soonest are betray'd.

KING FERDINAND - How! can that fair Hand acquaint it self with Death?
What wilt thou do, Florella?

FLORELLA - Your Destiny divert,
And give my Heart those Wounds design'd for yours.
If you advance, I'll give the deadly Blow.

KING FERDINAND - Hold! I command thee hold thy impious Hand,
My Heart dwells there, and if you strike, I die.

Enter Queen, Alonzo, and Elvira.

QUEEN ISABELLA - Florella! arm'd against the King?
[Snatches the Dagger and stabs her: the King rises.
Oh Traitress!

KING FERDINAND - Hold, hold, inhuman Murdress;
What hast thou done, most barbarous of thy Sex!
[Takes Florella in his Arms.

QUEEN ISABELLA - Destroy'd thy Murdress, and my too fair Rival. [Aside.

KING FERDINAND - My Murdress! what Devil did inspire thee
With Thoughts so black and sinful? cou'd this fair Saint
Be guilty of a Murder? No, no, too cruel Mother,
With her Eyes, her charming lovely Eyes,
She might have kill'd, and her too virtuous Cruelty.
Oh my Florella! Sacred lovely Creature!

FLORELLA - My Death was kind, since it prevented yours,
And by that Hand, which sav'd mine from a Guilt.
[Points to the Queen.
That Dagger I receiv'd of Abdelazer,
To stab that Heart, he said, that lov'd me best;
But I design'd to overcome your Passion,
And then to have vanquish'd Abdelazer's Jealousy:
But finding you too faithful to be happy,
I did resolve to die and have my wish.
Farewel, my King, my Soul begins its flight,
And now is hovering in eternal Night.

[Dies.

KING FERDINAND - She's gone, she's gone, her sacred Soul is fled
To that Divinity, of which it is a part;
Too excellent to inhabit Earthly Bodies.

ALONZO - Oh, Sir, you grieve too much, for one so foul.

KING FERDINAND - What profane Breath was that pronounc'd her foul?
Thy Mother's Soul, though turn'd into a Cherubim,
Was black to hers. Oh, she was all divine.
Alonzo, was it thou? her Brother!

ALONZO - When she was good, I own'd that Title, Sir.

KING FERDINAND - Good! by all the Gods, she was as chaste as Vestals,
As Saints translated to Divine Abodes.
I offer'd her to be my Queen, Alonzo,
To share the growing Glories of my Youth;
But uncorrupted she my Crown contemn'd,
And on her Virtue's Guard stood thus defended.
[Alon. weeps.
Oh my Florella! let me here lie fix'd,
[Kneels.
And never rise, till I am cold and pale
As thou, fair Saint, art now. But sure
She cou'd not die; that noble generous Heart,
That arm'd with Love and Honour, did rebate
All the fierce Sieges of my amorous Flame,
Might sure defend it self against those Wounds
Given by a Woman's Hand, or rather 'twas a Devil's.
[Rises.
What dost thou merit for this Treachery?
Thou vilest of thy Sex
But thou'rt a thing I have miscall'd a Mother,
And therefore will not touch thee, live to suffer
By a more shameful way; but here she lies,
Whom I, though dead, must still adore as living.

ALONZO - Sir, pray retire, there's danger in your stay;
When I reflect upon this Night's Disorder,
And the Queen's Art to raise my Jealousy;
And after that my Sister's being murder'd,
I must believe there is some deeper Plot,
Something design'd against your sacred Person.

KING FERDINAND - Alonzo, raise the Court, I'll find it,
[Ex. Alonzo.
Tho 'twere hid within my Mother's Soul.

QUEEN ISABELLA - My gentle Son, pardon my kind mistake,

I did believe her arm'd against thy Life.

KING FERDINAND - Peace, Fury! Not ill boding Raven Shrieks,
Nor midnight Cries of murder'd Ghosts, are more
Ungrateful, than thy faint and dull Excuses.
Be gone! and trouble not the silent Griefs,
Which will insensibly decay my Life,
Till like a Marble Statue I am fixt,
Dropping continual Tears upon her Tomb.
[Kneels and weeps at Florella's Feet.

ABDELAZER - [Within]. Guard all the Chamber-Doors. Fire and Confusion
Consume the Spanish Dogs, was I for this
Sent to fetch back a Philip, and a Cardinal,
To have my Wife abus'd?

Enter Abdelazer.

QUEEN ISABELLA - Patience, dear Abdelazer.

ABDELAZER - Patience and I am Foes: where's my Florella?
The King! and in Florella's Bed-Chamber!
Florella dead too!
Rise, thou eternal Author of my Shame;
Gay thing, to you I speak, [King rises.
And thus throw off Allegiance.

QUEEN ISABELLA - Oh, stay your Fury, generous Abdelazer.

ABDELAZER - Away, fond Woman.
[Throws her from him.

KING FERDINAND - Villain, to me this Language?

ABDELAZER - To thee, young amorous King.
How at this dead and silent time of Night,
Durst you approach the Lodgings of my Wife?

KING FERDINAND - I scorn to answer thee.

ABDELAZER - I'll search it in thy Heart then.

[They fight, Queen and Elv. run out crying Treason.

KING FERDINAND - The Devil's not yet ready for his Soul,
And will not claim his due. Oh, I am wounded. [Falls.

ABDELAZER - No doubt on't, Sir, these are no Wounds of Love.

KING FERDINAND - Whate'er they be, you might have spar'd 'em now,
Since those Florella give me were sufficient:

And yet a little longer, fixing thus
Thou'dst seen me turn to Earth, without thy aid.
Florella! Florella! is thy Soul fled so far
It cannot answer me, and call me on?
And yet like dying Ecchoes in my Ears,
I hear thee cry, my Love. I come, I come, fair Soul.
Thus at thy Feet, my Heart shall bleeding lie.
Who since it liv'd for thee - for thee - will die. [Dies.

ABDELAZER - So, thou art gone, there was a King but now,
And now a senseless, dull, and breathless nothing.
[A noise of fighting without.
Enter Queen running.

QUEEN ISABELLA - Oh Heavens! my Son, the King, the King is kill'd!
Yet I must save his Murderer: Fly, my Moor;
Alonzo, Sir, assisted by some Friends,
Has set upon your Guards,
And with resistless Fury is making hither.

ABDELAZER - Let him come on.

Enter Alonzo and others, led in by Osmin, Zarrack, and Moors.

Oh, are you fast?
[Takes away their Swords.

ALONZO - What mean'st thou, Villain?

ABDELAZER - To put your Swords to better uses, Sir,
Than to defend the cause of Ravishers.

ALONZO - Oh Heavens, the King is murder'd!

ABDELAZER - Look on that Object,
Thy Sister and my Wife, who's doubly murder'd,
First in her spotless Honour, then her Life.

ALONZO - Heaven is more guilty than the King in this.

QUEEN ISABELLA - My Lords, be calm; and since your King is murder'd.
Think of your own dear Safeties; chuse a new King,
That may defend you from the Tyrant's Rage.

ALONZO - Who should we chuse? Prince Philip is our King.

ABDELAZER - By Heaven, but Philip shall not be my King;
Philip's a Bastard, and Traytor to his Country:
He braves us with an Army at our Walls,
Threatning the Kingdom with a fatal Ruin.
And who shall lead you forth to Conquest now,

But Abdelazer, whose Sword reap'd Victory,
As oft as 'twas unsheath'd? and all for Spain
How many Laurels has this Head adorn'd?
Witness the many Battles I have won;
In which I've emptied all my youthful Veins!
And all for Spain! Ungrateful of my Favours!
I do not boast my Birth,
Nor will not urge to you my Kingdom's Ruin;
But loss of Blood, and numerous Wounds receiv'd
And still for Spain!
And can you think, that after all my Toils,
I wou'd be still a Slave? to Bastard Philip too?
That dangerous Foe, who with the Cardinal,
Threatens with Fire and Sword. I'll quench those Flames,
Such an esteem I still preserve for Spain.

ALONZO - What means this long Harangue? what does it aim at?

ABDELAZER - To be Protector of the Crown of Spain,
Till we agree about a lawful Successor.

ALONZO - Oh Devil!

QUEEN ISABELLA - We are betray'd, and round beset with Horrors;
If we deny him this, the Power being his,
We're all undone, and Slaves unto his Mercy.
Besides - Oh, give me leave to blush when I declare,
That Philip is, as he has rendred him.
But I in love to you, love to my Spain,
Chose rather to proclaim my Infamy,
Than an ambitious Bastard should be crown'd.

ALONZO - Here's a fine Plot,
What Devil reigns in Woman, when she doats? [Aside.

RODERIGO - My Lords, I see no remedy but he must be Protector.

ALONZO - Oh, Treachery, have you so soon forgot
The noble Philip, and his glorious Heir,
The murder'd Ferdinand?
And, Madam, you so soon forgot a Mother's Name,
That you wou'd give him Power that kill'd your Son?

ABDELAZER - The Modesty wherewith I'll use that Power,
Shall let you see, I have no other Interest
But what's intirely Spain's. Restore their Swords,
And he amongst you all who is dissatisfy'd,
I set him free this minute.

ALONZO - I take thee at thy word
And instantly to Philip's Camp will fly.

[Exit.

ABDELAZER - By all the Gods my Ancestors ador'd,
But that I scorn the envying World shou'd think
I took delight in Blood, I wou'd not part so with you.
But you, my Lords, who value Spain's Repose,
Must for it instantly with me take Arms.
Prince Philip, and the Cardinal, now ride
Like Jove in Thunder; we in Storms must meet them.
To Arms! to Arms! and then to Victory,
Resolv'd to conquer, or resolv'd to die.

[Exeunt.

ACT IV.

SCENE I. Abdelazer's Tent.

Enter Abdelazer, Osmin bearing his Helmet of Feathers, Zarrack with his Sword and Truncheon.

ABDELAZER - Come, Osmin, arm me quickly; for the Day
Comes on apace, and the fierce Enemy
Will take advantages by our delay.

Enter Queen Isabella and Elvira.

QUEEN ISABELLA - Oh, my dear Moor!
The rude, exclaiming, ill-affected Multitude
(Tempestuous as the Sea) run up and down,
Some crying, kill the Bastard, some the Moor;
These for King Philip, those for Abdelazer.

ABDELAZER - Your Fears are idle, blow 'em into Air.
I rush'd amongst the thickest of their Crouds,
And with the awful Splendor of my Eyes,
Like the imperious Sun, dispers'd the Clouds.
But I must combat now a fiercer Foe,
The hot-brain'd Philip, and a jealous Cardinal.

QUEEN ISABELLA - And must you go, before I make you mine?

ABDELAZER - That's my Misfortune when I return with Victory,
And lay my Wreaths of Laurel at your Feet,
You shall exchange them for your glorious Fetters.

QUEEN ISABELLA - How canst thou hope for Victory, when their Numbers
So far exceed thy Powers?

ABDELAZER - What's wanting there, we must supply with Conduct.

I know you will not stop at any thing
That may advance our Interest, and Enjoyment.

QUEEN ISABELLA - Look back on what I have already done;
And after that look forward with Assurance.

ABDELAZER - You then (with only Women in your Train)
Must to the Camp, and to the Cardinal's Tent;
Tell him, your Love to him hath drawn you thither:
Then undermine his Soul, you know the way on't.
And sooth him into a Belief, that the best way
To gain your Heart, is to leave Philip's Interest;
Urge 'tis the Kingdom's safety, and your own;
And use your fiercest Threats, to draw him to a Peace with me;
Not that you love me, but for the Kingdom's good:
Then in a Tent which I will pitch on purpose,
Get him to meet me: He being drawn off,
Thousands of Bigots (who think to cheat the World
Into an Opinion, that fighting for the Cardinal is
A pious Work) will (when he leaves the Camp)
Desert it too.

QUEEN ISABELLA - I understand you, and more than I have time to be
Instructed in, I will perform; and possibly
Before you can begin, I'll end my Conquests.

ABDELAZER - 'Twill be a Victory worthy of your Beauty.
I must to Horse, farewel, my generous Mistress.

QUEEN ISABELLA - Farewel! and may thy Arms as happy prove,
As shall my Art, when it dissembles Love.

[Exeunt.

SCENE II. Philip's Tent.

Enter Philip, Alonzo, and Guards.

PHILIP - 'Tis a sad Story thou hast told, Alonzo;
Yet 'twill not make me shed one single Tear:
They must be all of Blood that I will offer
To my dear Brother's Ghost
But, gallant Friend, this Good his Ills have done,
To turn thee over to our juster Interest,
For thou didst love him once.

ALONZO - Whilst I believ'd him honest, and for my Sister's sake;
But since, his Crimes have made a Convert of me.

PHILIP - Gods! is it possible the Queen should countenance

His horrid Villanies?

ALONZO - Nay, worse than so,'tis thought she'll marry him.

PHILIP - Marry him! then here upon my Knees I vow,
[Kneels.
To shake all Duty from my Soul;
And all that Reverence Children owe a Parent,
Shall henceforth be converted into Hate. [Rises.
Damnation! marry him! Oh, I cou'd curse my Birth!
This will confirm the World in their Opinion,
That she's the worst of Women;
That I am basely born too, (as she gives it out)
That Thought alone does a just Rage inspire,
And kindles round my Heart an active Fire.

ALONZO - A Disobedience, Sir, to such a Parent,
Heaven must forgive the Sin, if this be one:
Yet do not, Sir, in Words abate that Fire,
Which will assist you a more effectual way.

PHILIP - Death! I could talk of it an Age;
And, like a Woman, fret my Anger high:
Till like my Rage, I have advanc'd my Courage,
Able to fight the World against my Mother.

ALONZO - Our Wrongs without a Rage, will make us fight,
Wrongs that wou'd make a Coward resolute.

PHILIP - Come, noble Youth,
Let us join both our several Wrongs in one,
And from them make a solemn Resolution,
Never to part our Interest, till this Moor,
This worse than Devil Moor be sent to Hell.

ALONZO - I do.

PHILIP - Hark, hark, the Charge is sounded, let's to Horse,
St. Jaques for the Right of Spain and me.

[Exeunt.

SCENE III. A Grave.

Drums and Trumpets afar off, with noise of fighting at a distance: After a little while, enter Philip in a Rage.

PHILIP - Oh unjust Powers! why d'ye protect this Monster?
And this damn'd Cardinal, that comes not up
With the Castilian Troops? curse on his formal Politicks

Enter Alonzo.
Alonzo, where's the Moor?

ALONZO - The Moor, a Devil, never did Fiend of Hell,
Compell'd by some Magician's Charms,
Break thro the Prison of the folded Earth
With more swift Horrour, than this Prince of Fate
Breaks thro our Troops in spite of Opposition.

PHILIP - Death! 'tis not his single Arm that works the Wonders,
But our Cowardice. Oh, this Dog Cardinal!

Enter Antonio.

ANTONIO - Sound a Retreat, or else the Day is lost.

PHILIP - I'll beat that Cur to Death that sounds Retreat.

Enter Sebastian.

SEBASTIAN - Sound a Retreat.

PHILIP - Who is't that tempts my Sword? continue the Alarm,
Fight on Pell-mell, fight, kill, be damn'd, do any thing
But sound Retreat. Oh, this damn'd Coward Cardinal!
[Exeunt.

The noise of fighting near; after a little while enter Philip again.

PHILIP - Not yet, ye Gods! Oh, this eternal Coward!

Enter Alonzo.

ALONZO - Sir, bring up your Reserves, or all is lost;
Ambition plumes the Moor, that makes him act
Deeds of such Wonder, that even you wou'd envy them.

PHILIP - 'Tis well, I'll raise my Glories to that dazling height,
Shall darken his, or set in endless Night.

[Exeunt.

SCENE IV. A Grove.

Enter Cardinal Mendozo and Queen Isabella; the noise of a Battel continuing afar off all the Scene.

QUEEN ISABELLA - By all thy Love, by all thy Languishments,
By all those Sighs and Tears paid to my Cruelty,
By all thy Vows, thy passionate Letters sent,
I do conjure thee, go not forth to fight:

Command your Troops not to engage with Philip,
Who aims at nothing but the Kingdom's ruin.
Fernando's kill'd - the Moor has gain'd the Power,
A Power that you nor Philip can withstand;
And is't not better he were lost than Spain,
Since one must be a Sacrifice?
Besides, if I durst tell it,
There's something I cou'd whisper to thy Soul,
Wou'd make thee blush at ev'ry single Good
Thou'ast done that insolent Boy; But 'tis not now
A time for Stories of so strange a Nature,
Which when you know, you will conclude with me,
That every Man that arms for Philip's Cause,
Merits the name of Traitor.
Be wise in time, and leave his shameful Interest,
An Interest thou wilt curse thy self for taking;
Be wise, and make Alliance with the Moor.

CARDINAL MENDOZO - And, Madam, should I lay aside my Wrongs,
Those publick Injuries I have receiv'd,
And make a mean and humble Peace with him?
No, let Spain be ruin'd by our Civil Swords,
E'er for its safety I forego mine Honour.

Enter an Officer.

OFFICER - Advance, Sir, with your Troops, or we are lost.

CARDINAL MENDOZO - Give order

QUEEN ISABELLA - That they stir not on their Lives;
Is this the Duty that you owe your Country?
Is this your Sanctity and Love to me?
Is't thus you treat the Glory I have offer'd
To raise you to my Bed?
To rule a Kingdom, be a Nation's Safety,
To advance in hostile manner to their Walls;
Walls that confine your Countrymen, and Friends,
And Queen, to whom you've vow'd eternal Peace,
Eternal Love? And will you court in Arms?
Such rude Addresses wou'd but ill become you.
No, from this hour renounce all Claims to me,
Or Philip's Interest; for let me tell you, Cardinal,
This Love, and that Revenge, are inconsistent.

CARDINAL MENDOZO - But, Madam

QUEEN ISABELLA - No more disband your Rebel Troops,
And strait with me to Abdelazer's Tent,
Where all his Claims he shall resign to you,
Both in my self, the Kingdom, and the Crown:

You being departed, thousands more will leave him,
And you're alone the Prop to his Rebellion.

Enter Sebastian.

SEBASTIAN - Advance, advance, my Lord, with all your Force,
Or else the Prince and Victory is lost,
Which now depends upon his single Valour;
Who, like some ancient Hero, or some God,
Thunders amongst the thickest of his Enemies,
Destroying all before him in such numbers,
That Piles of Dead obstruct his passage to the living
Relieve him strait, my Lord, with our last Cavalry and
Hopes.

CARDINAL MENDOZO - I'll follow instantly.
[Ex. Sebastian.

QUEEN ISABELLA - Sir, but you shall not, unless it be to Death
Shall you preserve the only Man I hate,
And hate with so much reason? let him fall
A Victim to an injur'd Mother's Honour.
Come, I will be obey'd, indeed I must [Fawns on him.

CARDINAL MENDOZO - When you're thus soft, can I retain my Anger?
Oh, look but ever thus in spite of Injuries
I shall become as tame and peaceable,
As are your charming Eyes, when dress'd in Love,
Which melting down my Rage, leave me defenceless.
Ah, Madam, have a generous care of me,
For I have now resign'd my Power to you.

[Shouts within.

QUEEN ISABELLA - What Shouts are these?

Enter Sebastian.

SEBASTIAN - My Lord, the Enemy is giving ground,
And Philip's Arm alone sustains the day:
Advance, Sir, and compleat the Victory.
[Exit.

QUEEN ISABELLA - Give order strait, that a Retreat be sounded;
And whilst they do so, by me conducted,
We'll instantly to Abdelazer's Tent
Haste, haste, my Lord, whilst I attend you here.
[Ex. severally.
[Cardinal going out, is met by Philip.

PHILIP - Oh, damn your lazy Order, where have you been, Sir?

But 'tis no time for Questions,
Move forward with your Reserves.

CARDINAL MENDOZO - I will not, Sir.

PHILIP - How, will not!

CARDINAL MENDOZO - Now to advance would be impolitick;
Already by your desperate Attempts,
You've lost the best part of our Hopes.

PHILIP - Death! you lye.

CARDINAL MENDOZO - Lye, Sir!

PHILIP - Yes, lye, Sir, therefore come on,
Follow the desperate Reer-Guard, which is mine,
And where I'll die, or conquer, follow my Sword
The bloody way it leads, or else, by Heaven,
I'll give the Moor the Victory in spite,
And turn my Force on thee
Plague of your Cowardice. Come, follow me.

[Ex. Cardinal.

SCENE V. The Grove.

As Philip is going off, he is overtook by Alonzo, Antonio, Sebastian, and other Officers: At the other side some Moors, and other of Abdelazer's Party, enter and fall on Philip and the rest, the Moors are beaten off, one left dead on the Stage.

Enter Abdelazer, with Roderigo and some others.

ABDELAZER - Oh, for more Work, more Souls to send to Hell!
Ha, ha, ha, here's one going thither, Sirrah, Slave
Moor, who kill'd thee? how he grins, this Breast,
Had it been temper'd and made proof like mine,
It never wou'd have been a Mark for Fools.

Abdelazer going out: Enter Philip, Alonzo, Sebastian, Antonio, and Officers, as passing over the Stage.

PHILIP - I'll wear my Sword to th' Hilt, but I will find
The Subject of my Vengeance.
Moor, 'tis for thee I seek, where art thou, Slave?

ABDELAZER - Here, Philip. [Abd. turns.

PHILIP - Fate and Revenge, I thank thee.

ABDELAZER - Why, thou art brave, whoe'er begot thee.

PHILIP - Villain, a King begot me.

ABDELAZER - I know not that,
But I'll be sworn thy Mother was a Queen,
And I will kill thee handsomly for her sake.

[Offers to fight, their Parties hinder them.

ALONZO - Hold, hold, my Prince.

OSMIN - Great Sir, what mean you? [To Abd.
The Victory being yours, to give your Life away
On one so mad and desperate.
[Their Parties draw.

PHILIP - Alonzo, hold,
We two will be the Fate of this great Day.

ABDELAZER - And I'll forego all I've already won,
And claim no Conquest; the whole heaps of Bodies,
Which this Right-hand has slain, declare me Victor.

PHILIP - No matter who's the Victor; I have thee in my view,
And will not leave thee,
Till thou hast crown'd those Heaps, and made 'em all
The glorious Trophies of my Victory. Come on, Sir.

ALONZO - You shall not fight thus single;
If you begin, by Heaven, we'll all fall on.

PHILIP - Dost thou suspect my Power?
Oh, I am arm'd with more than compleat Steel,
The Justice of my Quarrel; when I look
Upon my Father's Wrongs, my Brother's Wounds,
My Mother's Infamy, Spain's Misery,
I am all Fire; and yet I am too cold
To let out Blood enough for my Revenge:
Therefore stir not a Sword on my side.

ABDELAZER - Nor on mine.

They fight; both their Parties engage on either side; the Scene draws off, and discovers both the Armies, which all fall on and make the main Battel: Philip prevails, the Moors give ground: Then the Scene closes to the the Grove. Enter some Moors flying in disorder.

SCENE VI. Changes to a Tent.

Enter Abdelazer, Roderigo, Osmin, Zarrack, and some others of his Party.

RODERIGO - Oh, fly, my Lord, fly, for the Day is lost.

ABDELAZER - There are three hundred and odd Days i'th Year,
And cannot we lose one? dismiss thy Fears,
They'll make a Coward of thee.

OSMIN - Sir, all the noble Spaniards have forsook you;
Your Soldiers faint, are round beset with Enemies,
Nor can you shun your Fate, but by your Flight.

ABDELAZER - I can and must in spite of Fate:
The Wheel of War shall turn about again,
And dash the Current of his Victories.
This is the Tent I've pitched, at distance from the Armies,
To meet the Queen and Cardinal;
Charm'd with the Magick of Dissimulation,
I know by this h'as furl'd his Ensigns up,
And is become a tame and coward Ass.
[A Retreat is sounded.
Hark, hark, 'tis done: oh, my inchanting Engine!
Dost thou not hear Retreat sounded?

RODERIGO - Sure 'tis impossible.

ABDELAZER - She has prevail'd, a Woman's Tongue and Eyes
Are Forces stronger than Artilleries.
Enter Queen, Cardinal, Women, and Soldiers.
We are betray'd.

QUEEN ISABELLA - What means this Jealousy? lay by your Weapons.
And embrace, the sight of these beget Suspicion:
Abdelazer, by my Birth he comes in peace;
Lord Cardinal, on my Honour so comes he.

ABDELAZER - Let him withdraw his Troops then.

QUEEN ISABELLA - They're Guards for all our Safeties:
Give me your Hand, Prince Cardinal, thine, Abdelazer
[She brings them together, they embrace.
This blest Accord I do behold with Joy.

CARDINAL - Abdelazer,
I at the Queen's Command have met you here,
To know what 'tis you will propose to us.

ABDELAZER - Peace and eternal Friendship 'twixt us two.
How much against my Will I took up Arms,
Be witness, Heav'n: nor was it in revenge to you,
But to let out th' infected Blood of Philip,
Whose sole aim
Is to be King, which Spain will never suffer;

Spain gave me Education, though not Birth,
Which has intitled it my native Home,
To which such Reverence and Esteem I bear,
I will preserve it from the Tyrant's Rage.
The People who once lov'd him, now abhor him,
And 'tis your Power alone that buoys him up:
And when you've lifted him into a Throne,
'Tis time to shake you off.

CARDINAL MENDOZO - Whilst I behold him as my native Prince,
My Honour and Religion bids me serve him;
Yet not when I'm convinc'd that whilst I do so,
I injure Spain.

ABDELAZER - If he were so, the Powers above forbid
We should not serve, adore, and fight for him;
But Philip is a Bastard: nay, 'twill surprize ye,
But that 'tis Truth, the Queen will satisfy you.

QUEEN ISABELLA - With one bold Word he has undone my Honour.
[Weeps.
Too bluntly, Abdelazer, you repeat
That which by slow Degrees you shou'd have utter'd.

ABDELAZER - Pardon my Roughness, Madam, I meant well.

Card. Philip a Bastard!
If by such Arts you wou'd divide me from him,
I shall suspect you wou'd betray us both.

QUEEN ISABELLA - Sir, he informs you Truth; and I blush less
To own him so, than that he is a Traitor.

Card. Philip a Bastard! oh, it cannot be
Madam, take heed you do not for Revenge,
Barter your dearer Honour, and lose both.

QUEEN ISABELLA - I know what's due to Honour, and Revenge,
But better what I owe to Spain, and you
You are a Prince o'th' Blood, and may put off
The Cardinal when you please, and be a Monarch.

CARDINAL MENDOZO - Though my Ambition's equal to my Passion,
Neither shall make me act against those Principles
My Honour ever taught me to obey.
And, Madam
'Tis less a Sin, not to believe you her,
Than 'tis to doubt your Virtue.

QUEEN ISABELLA - I wish it were untold, if it must forfeit
The least of your Esteem but that 'tis Truth,

Be witness, Heav'n, my Shame, my Sighs, and Tears.
[Weeps.

CARDINAL MENDOZO - Why, Madam, was't so long conceal'd from me?

QUEEN ISABELLA - The Circumstances I shall at leisure tell you:
And for the present,
Let it suffice, he cannot rule in Spain,
Nor can you side with him, without being made
As much incapable to reign as he.

CARDINAL MENDOZO - Though Love and Honour I have always made
The Business of my Life;
My Soul retains too so much of Ambition,
As puts me still in mind of what I am,
A Prince, and Heir to Spain:
Nor shall my blinded Zeal to Loyalty,
Make me that glorious Interest resign,
Since Philip's Claims are not so great as mine.
Madam, tho I'm convinc'd I've done amiss
In taking Arms for Philip,
Yet 'twill be difficult to disengage my self.

ABDELAZER - Most easily
Proclaim it in the head of all your Troops,
The Justice of your Cause for leaving him;
And tell 'em, 'tis a Work of Piety
To follow your Example.
The giddy Rout are guided by Religion,
More than by Justice, Reason, or Allegiance.
The Crown which I as a good Husband keep,
I will lay down upon the empty Throne;
Marry you the Queen, and fill it and for me,
I'll ever pay you Duty as a Subject.
[Bows low.

CARDINAL MENDOZO - On these Conditions all I am is yours;
Philip we cannot fear, all he can do
Is to retire for refuge into Portugal.

ABDELAZER - That wou'd be dangerous
Is there no Arts to get him in our Power?

CARDINAL MENDOZO - Perhaps by Policy, and seeming Friendship,
For we have reason yet to fear his Force;
And since I'm satisfy'd he's not my lawful Prince,
I cannot think it an Impiety
To sacrifice him to the Peace of Spain,
And every Spirit that loves Liberty:
First we'll our Forces join, and make 'em yours,
Then give me your Authority to arrest him;

If so we can surprize him, we'll spare the hazard
Of a second Battel.

ABDELAZER - My Lord, retire into my inner Tent,
And all things shall be instantly perform'd.

[Exeunt all.

SCENE VII. The Grove.

Enter some of Philip's Party running over the Stage, pursued by Philip, Alonzo, Sebastian, Antonio, and some few Officers more.

ALONZO - Do not pursue 'em, Sir, such coward Slaves
Deserve not Death from that illustriate Hand.

PHILIP - Eternal Plagues consume 'em in their flight;
Oh, this damn'd coward Cardinal has betray'd us!
When all our Swords were nobly dy'd in Blood,
When with red Sweat that trickled from our Wounds
We'ad dearly earn'd the long disputed Victory,
Then to lose all, then to sound base Retreat,
It swells my Anger up to perfect Madness.

ALONZO - Indeed 'twas wondrous strange.

SEBASTIAN - I'm glad, Sir

PHILIP - Art glad of it? art glad we are abandon'd?
That I, and thou have lost the hopeful'st Day

SEBASTIAN - Great Sir, I'm glad that you came off alive.

PHILIP - Thou hast a lean Face and a carrion Heart
A plague upon the Moor, and thee. Oh, Alonzo,
To run away, follow'd by all the Army!
Oh, I cou'd tear my Hair, and curse my Soul to Air!
Cardinal, thou Traitor, Judas, that would'st sell
Thy God again, as thou hast done thy Prince.
But come, we're yet a few,
And we will fight till there be left but one
If I prove him, I'll die a glorious death.
Ant. Yes, but the Cardinal has took pious Care
It shall be in our Beds.

SEBASTIAN - We are as bad as one already, Sir; for all our Fellows are crawl'd home, some with ne'er a Leg, others with ne'er a Arm, some with their Brains beat out, and glad they escaped so.

PHILIP - But, my dear Countrymen, you'll stick to me.

1st SOLDIER - Ay, wou'd I were well off [Aside.

PHILIP - Speak, stout Sceva, wilt thou not?

1st SOLDIER - Sceva, Sir, who's that?

PHILIP - A gallant Roman, that fought by Caesar's side,
Till all his Body cover'd o'er with Arrows,
Shew'd like a monstrous Porcupine.

1st SOLDIER - And did he die, Sir?

PHILIP - He wou'd not but have dy'd for Caesar's Empire.

1st SOLDIER - Hah, why, Sir, I'm none of Sceva, but honest Diego, yet would as willingly die as he, but that I have a Wife and Children; and if I die they beg.

PHILIP - For every drop of Blood which thou shalt lose,
I'll give thy Wife, a Diadem.

1st SOLDIER - Stark mad, as I am valiant!

Enter Cardinal Mendozo, Officers and Soldiers: Philip offers to run on him, is held by Alonzo.

PHILIP - Oh Heav'n! is not that the Cardinal?
Traitor, how dar'st thou tempt my Rage, and Justice?

CARDINAL MENDOZO - Your Pardon, Sir, I come in humble Love
To offer happy Peace.

PHILIP - Was that thy aim when base Retreat was sounded?
Oh, thou false Cardinal, let me go, Alonzo
Death! offer happy Peace! no, offer War,
Bring Fire and Sword. Hell and Damnation - Peace!
Oh, damn your musty Peace. No, will you fight and cry,
Down with the Moor! and then I'll die in peace.
I have a Heart, two Arms, a Soul, a Head,
I'll hazard these I can but hazard all
Come, I will kneel to thee and be thy Slave
[Kneels.
I'll let thee tread on me, do any thing,
So this damn'd Moor may fall.

CARDINAL MENDOZO - Yes, Sir, he shall

PHILIP - Gods! shall he, thy noble Hand upon't,
And for this Promise, take my grateful Heart.

[Embraces him.
Shall Abdelazer fall?

CARDINAL MENDOZO - Yes, upon thee
Like the tall Ruins of a falling Tower,
To crush thee into Dust
[As they embrace, the Guards seize him and the rest.
Traitor and Bastard, I arrest thee of High-Treason.

PHILIP - Hah! Traitor! and Bastard and from thee!
[They hold Philip's Hands.

CARDINAL MENDOZO - Guards, to your Hands the Prisoner is committed.
There's your Warrant. Alonzo, you are free.
[Ex. Cardinal.

PHILIP - Prithee lend me one Hand to wipe my Eyes,
And see who 'tis dares authorize this Warrant:
The Devil and his Dam! the Moor and Queen!
Their Warrant! Gods! Alonzo, must we obey it?
Villains, you cannot be my Jailors; there's no Prison,
No Dungeon deep enough; no Gate so strong,
To keep a Man confin'd so mad with Wrong.
Oh, dost thou weep, Alonzo?

ALONZO - I wou'd fain shed a Tear,
But from my Tears so many Show'rs are gone,
They are too poor to pay your Sorrow's Tribute;
There is no Remedy, we must to Prison.

PHILIP - Yes, and from thence to Death
I thought I should have had a Tomb hung round
With tatter'd Ensigns, broken Spears and Javelins;
And that my Body, with a thousand Wounds,
Shou'd have been borne on some triumphant Chariot,
With solemn Mourning, Drums, and Trumpets sounding;
Whilst all the wondring World with Grief and Envy,
Had wish'd my glorious Destiny their own:
But now, Alonzo, like a Beast I fall,
And hardly Pity waits my Funeral.

[Exeunt.

ACT V.

SCENE I. A Presence-Chamber, with a Throne and Canopy.

Enter Abdelazer, Cardinal, Alonzo, Ordonio, Roderigo, and other Lords, one bearing the Crown, which is laid on the Table on a Cushion; the Queen, Leonora, and Ladies.

They all seat themselves, leaving the Throne and Chair of State empty. Abdelazer rises and bows, Roderigo kneeling, presents him with the Crown.

ABDELAZER - Grandees of Spain, if in this royal Presence
There breathes a Man, who having laid his hold
So fast on such a Jewel, and dares wear it,
In the Contempt of Envy, as I dare;
Yet uncompell'd (as freely as the Gods
Bestow their Blessings) wou'd give such Wealth away;
Let such a Man stand forth, are ye all fix'd?
No wonder, since a King's a Deity.
And who'd not be a God?
This glorious Prospect, when I first saw the Light,
Met with my Infant Hopes; nor have those Fetters
(Which e'er they grew towards Men, Spain taught me how to wear)
Made me forget what's due to that illustrious Birth;
Yet thus I cast aside the Rays of Majesty

[Kneels, and lays the Crown on the Table.

And on my Knee do humbly offer up
This splendid powerful thing, and ease your Fears
Of Usurpation and of Tyranny.

ALONZO - What new Device is this? [Aside.

CARDINAL MENDOZO - This is an Action generous and just
Let us proceed to new Election.

ABDELAZER - Stay, Peers of Spain,
If young Prince Philip be King Philip's Son,
Then is he Heir to Philip, and his Crown;
But if a Bastard, then he is a Rebel,
And as a Traitor to the Crown shou'd bleed:
That dangerous popular Spirit must be laid,
Or Spain must languish under civil Swords;
And Portugal taking advantage of those Disorders,
(Assisted by the Male-contents within,
If Philip live) will bring Confusion home.
Our Remedy for this is first to prove,
And then proclaim him Bastard.

ALONZO - That Project wou'd be worth your Politicks [Aside.
How shou'd we prove him Bastard?

ABDELAZER - Her Majesty being lately urg'd by Conscience,
And much above her Honour prizing Spain,
Declar'd this Secret, but has not nam'd the Man;
If he be noble and a Spaniard born,
He shall repair her Fame by marrying her.

CARDINAL MENDOZO - No; Spaniard, or Moor, the daring Slave shall die.

QUEEN ISABELLA - Would I were cover'd with a Veil of Night,
[Weeps.
That I might hide the Blushes on my Cheeks!
But when your Safety comes into Dispute,
My Honour, nor my Life must come in competition.
I'll therefore hide my Eyes, and blushing own,
That Philip's Father is i'th' Presence now.

ALONZO - I'th' Presence! name him.

QUEEN ISABELLA - The Cardinal
[All rise in Amazement.

CARDINAL MENDOZO - How's this, Madam!

ABDELAZER - How! the Cardinal!

CARDINAL MENDOZO - I Philip's Father, Madam!

QUEEN ISABELLA - Dull Lover, is not all this done for thee!
Dost thou not see a Kingdom and my self,
By this Confession, thrown into thy Arms?

CARDINAL MENDOZO - On Terms so infamous I must despise it.

QUEEN ISABELLA - Have I thrown by all Sense of Modesty,
To render you the Master of my Bed,
To be refus'd, was there any other way?

CARDINAL MENDOZO - I cannot yield; this Cruelty transcends
All you have ever done me. Heavens! what a Contest
Of Love and Honour swells my rising Heart!

QUEEN ISABELLA - By all my Love, if you refuse me now,
Now when I have remov'd all Difficulties,
I'll be reveng'd a thousand killing ways.

CARDINAL MENDOZO - Madam, I cannot own so false a thing,
My Conscience and Religion will not suffer me.

QUEEN ISABELLA - Away with all this Canting; Conscience, and Religion!
No, take advice from nothing but from Love.

CARDINAL MENDOZO - 'Tis certain I'm bewitch'd, she has a Spell
Hid in those charming Lips.

ALONZO - Prince Cardinal, what say you to this?

CARDINAL MENDOZO - I cannot bring it forth

QUEEN ISABELLA - Do't, or thou'rt lost for ever.

CARDINAL MENDOZO - Death! What's a Woman's Power!
And yet I can resist it.

QUEEN ISABELLA - And dare you disobey me?

CARDINAL MENDOZO - Is't not enough I've given you up my Power,
Nay, and resign'd my Life into your Hands,
But you wou'd damn me too, I will not yield
Oh, now I find a very Hell within me;
How am I misguided by my Passion!

ALONZO - Sir, we attend your Answer.

QUEEN ISABELLA - 'Tis now near twenty Years, when newly married,
(And 'tis the Custom here to marry young,)
King Philip made a War in Barbary,
Won Tunis, conquer'd Fez, and hand to hand
Slew great Abdela, King of Fez, and Father
To this Barbarian Prince.

ABDELAZER - I was but young, and yet I well remember
My Father's Wound, poor Barbary but no more.

QUEEN ISABELLA - In absence of my King I liv'd retir'd,
Shut up in my Apartment with my Women,
Suffering no Visits, but the Cardinal's,
To whom the King had left me as his Charge;
But he, unworthy of that Trust repos'd,
Soon turned his Business into Love.

CARDINAL MENDOZO - Heavens! how will this Story end? [Aside.

QUEEN ISABELLA - A Tale, alas! unpleasant to my Ear,
And for the which I banish'd him my Presence,
But oh, the power of Gold! he bribes my Women,
That they should tell me (as a Secret too)
The King (whose Wars were finish'd) would return
Without acquainting any with the time;
He being as jealous, as I was fair and young,
Meant to surprize me in the dead of Night:
This pass'd upon my Youth, which ne'er knew Art.

CARDINAL MENDOZO - Gods! is there any Hell but Woman's Falshood! [Aside.

QUEEN ISABELLA - The following Night I hasted to my Bed,
To wait my expected Bliss, nor was it long
Before his gentle Steps approach'd my Ears.

Undress'd he came, and with a vigorous haste
Flew to my yielding Arms: I call'd him King,
My dear lov'd Lord; and in return he breath'd
Into my Bosom, in soft gentle Whispers,
My Queen! my Angel! my lov'd Isabella!
And at that word, I need not tell the rest.

ALONZO - What's all this, Madam, to the Cardinal?

QUEEN ISABELLA - Ah, Sir, the Night too short for his Caresses,
Made room for Day, Day that betray'd my Shame;
For in my guilty Arms I found the Cardinal.

ALONZO - Madam, why did not you complain of this?

QUEEN ISABELLA - Alas, I was but young, and full of Fears;
Bashful, and doubtful of a just Belief,
Knowing King Philip's rash and jealous Temper;
But from your Justice I expect Revenge.

RODERIGO - His Crime, my Lords, is Death, by all our Laws.

CARDINAL MENDOZO - Have you betray'd me by my too much Faith?
Oh shameless Creature, am I disarm'd for this?
Had I but so much Ease to be inrag'd,
Sure I shou'd kill thee for this Treachery:
But I'm all Shame, and Grief. By all that's holy,
My Lords, I never did commit this Crime.

ABDELAZER - 'Tis but in vain, Prince Cardinal, to deny it.

QUEEN ISABELLA - Do not believe him, Lords;
Revenge, let Sentence pass upon the Traitor.

CARDINAL MENDOZO - I own that Name with Horror, which you drew me to,
When I betray'd the best of Men, and Princes;
And 'tis but just you fit me for Despairs,
That may instruct me how to follow him in Death:
Yet as I'm Prince o'th' Blood, and Cardinal too,
You cannot be my Judges.

ABDELAZER - You shall be try'd, Sir, as becomes your Quality.
Osmin, we commit the Cardinal to your Charge.

CARDINAL MENDOZO - Heaven! should I live to that! No,
I have within me a private Shame,
That shall secure me from the publick one.

ALONZO - A pretty turn of State! we shall all follow, Sir.

CARDINAL MENDOZO - The Powers above are just:

Thus I my Prince a Sacrifice first made,
And now my self am on the Altar laid.

[Ex. Cardinal, guarded.

ABDELAZER - Madam, retire, you've acted so divinely,
You've fill'd my Soul with new admiring Passion:
I'll wait on you in your Apartment instantly,
And at your Feet pay all my Thanks, and Love.

QUEEN ISABELLA - Make haste, my dearest Moor, whilst I retire,
And fit my Soul to meet thy kind Desire.

[Ex. Queen and her Train; Leonara, advancing to follow, is staid by Abdelazer.

ABDELAZER - Stay, beauteous Maid, stay, and receive that Crown,
[Leads her back.
Which as your due, Heav'n and all Spain present you with.

ALONZO - But granting Philip is that thing you call him,
If we must grant him so, who then shall reign?
Not that we do not know who ought to reign,
But ask who 'tis you will permit to do so. [To Abdelazer.

ABDELAZER - Who but bright Leonora! the Royal Off-spring
Of noble Philip, whose Innocence and Beauty,
Without th' advantage of her glorious Birth,
Merits all Adoration.

ALL - With Joy we do salute her Queen.

ABDELAZER - Live Leonora! beauteous Queen of Spain!
[Shout.

ALONZO - From Abdelazer this! it cannot be,
At least not real. [Aside.

ABDELAZER - My Lords,
Be it now your Care magnificently to provide
Both for the Coronation, and the Marriage
Of the fair Queen;
Let nothing be omitted that may shew,
How we can pay, where we so vastly owe.
[Bows.

ALONZO - I am much bound to Spain, and you, my Lords,
For this great Condescenion.

LEONORA - My Lords, I thank ye all,
And most the gallant Moor, I am not well
[Turns to Alon.

Something surrounds my Heart so full of Death,
I must retire to give my Sorrow Breath.

[Ex. Leonora followed by all but Abdelazer and Roderigo who looks on Abdelazer.

RODERIGO - Sir, what have you done?

ABDELAZER - What every Man that loves like me shou'd do;
Undone my self for ever, to beget
One Moment's thought in her, that I adore her;
That she may know, none ever lov'd like me,
I've thrown away the Diadem of Spain
'Tis gone! and there's no more to set but this
(My Heart) at all, and at this one last Cast,
Sweep up my former Losses, or be undone.

RODERIGO - You court at a vast Rate, Sir.

ABDELAZER - Oh, she's a Goddess! a Creature made by Heaven
To make my prosperous Toils all sweet and charming!
She must be Queen, I and the Gods decree it.

RODERIGO - Sir, is she not designed Alonzo's Bride?

ABDELAZER - Yes, so her self and he have ill agreed;
But Heav'n and I am of another Mind,
And must be first obey'd.

RODERIGO - Alonzo will not yield his Interest easily.

ABDELAZER - Wou'd that were all my stop to Happiness;
But, Roderigo, this fond amorous Queen
Sits heavy on my Heart.

RODERIGO - She's but a Woman, nor has more Lives than one.

ABDELAZER - True, Roderigo, and thou hast dealt in Murders,
And knowest the safest way to

RODERIGO - How, Sir!

ABDELAZER - Thou dar'st not sure pretend to any Virtue;
Had Hell inspir'd thee with less Excellency
Than Arts of killing Kings, thou'dst ne'er been rais'd
To that exalted Height, t' have known my Secrets.

RODERIGO - But, Sir

ABDELAZER - Slave, look back upon the Wretchedness I took thee from;
What Merits had thou to deserve my Bounty,
But Vice, brave prosperous Vice?

Thou'rt neither wise, nor valiant.

RODERIGO - I own my self that Creature rais'd by you,
And live but to repay you, name the way.

ABDELAZER - My business is to have the Queen remov'd;
She does expect my coming this very Hour;
And when she does so, 'tis her Custom to be retir'd,
Dismissing all attendance, but Elvira.

RODERIGO - The rest I need not be instructed in.

[Ex. Roderigo.

Enter Osmin.

OSMIN - The Cardinal, Sir, is close confin'd with Philip.

ABDELAZER - 'Tis well.

OSMIN - And do you think it fit, Sir, they shou'd live?

ABDELAZER - No, this day they both must die, some sort of Death,
That may be thought was given them by themselves:
I'm sure I give them cause, Osmin, view well this Ring;
Whoever brings this Token to your Hands,
Without considering Sex, or Quality,
Let 'em be kill'd.

OSMIN - Your Will shall be obey'd in every thing.

[Exeunt severally.

SCENE II. A fine Chamber. A Table and Chair.

Enter Queen Isabella and Elvira.

QUEEN ISABELLA - Elvira, hast thou drest my Lodgings up,
Fit to receive my Moor?
Are they all gay, as Altars, when some Monarch
Is there to offer up rich Sacrifices?
Hast thou strew'd all the Floor his Feet must press,
With the soft new-born Beauties of the Spring?

ELVIRA - Madam, I've done as you commanded me.

QUEEN ISABELLA - Let all the Chambers too be fill'd with Lights;
There's a Solemnity methinks in Night,
That does insinuate Love into the Soul,
And make the bashful Lover more assur'd.

ELVIRA - Madam,
You speak as if this were your first Enjoyment.

QUEEN ISABELLA - My first! Oh Elvira, his Power, like his Charms,
His Wit, or Bravery, every hour renews;
Love gathers Sweets like Flow'rs, which grow more fragrant,
The nearer they approach Maturity.
[Knock.
Hark! 'tis my Moor, give him admittance strait,
The Thought comes o'er me like a gentle Gale,
Raising my Blood into a thousand Curls.

ELVIRA - Madam, it is a Priest

QUEEN ISABELLA - A Priest! Oh, send him quickly hence;
I wou'd not have so cold and dull an Object,
Meet with my nobler Sense, 'tis mortifying.

ELVIRA - Perhaps 'tis some Petition from the Cardinal.

QUEEN ISABELLA - Why, what have I to do with Priest or Cardinal?
Let him not enter

[Elvira. goes out, and returns with Roderigo drest like a Fryar.

ELVIRA - From Abdelazer, Madam.

QUEEN ISABELLA - H'as named a Word will make all Places free.

RODERIGO - Madam, be pleas'd to send your Woman hence,
I've something to deliver from the Moor,
Which you alone must be acquainted with.

QUEEN ISABELLA - Well, your Formality shall be allowed, retire
[To Elvira Exit Elvira.
What have you to deliver to me now?

RODERIGO - This -

[Shews a Dagger, and takes her roughly by the Hands.

QUEEN ISABELLA - Hah!

RODERIGO - You must not call for help, unless to Heaven.

QUEEN ISABELLA - What daring thing art thou?

RODERIGO - One that has now no time to answer thee.

[Stabs her, she struggles, her Arm bleeds.

QUEEN ISABELLA - Oh, hold thy killing Hand! I am thy Queen.

RODERIGO - Thou may'st be Devil too, for ought I know;
I'll try thy Substance thus
[Stabs again.

QUEEN ISABELLA - Oh, Abdelazer!
Thou hast well reveng'd me, on my Sins of Love;
[He seats her in the Chair.
But shall I die thus tamely unrcveng'd?
Help - murder - help -
[He offers to stab again.

Enter Elvira, and other Women.

ELVIRA - Oh Heavens! the Queen is murder'd, help the Queen!

[Roderigo offers to stab Elvira

Enter Abdelazer.

ABDELAZER - Hah! the Queen! what sacrilegious Hand,
Or Heart so brutal
Durst thus profane the Shrine ador'd by me?
Guard well the Passages.

QUEEN ISABELLA - Thou art that sacrilegious, brutal thing!
And false as are the Deities thou worship'st.

ABDELAZER - Gods! let me not understand that killing Language?
Inform me quickly, how you came thus wounded,
Lest looking on that sacred Stream of Blood,
I die e'er I've reveng'd you on your Murderer.

QUEEN ISABELLA - Haste then, and kill thy self; thou art my Murderer.
Nor had his Hand, if not by thee instructed,
Aim'd at a Sin so dangerous

ABDELAZER - Surely she'll live [Aside.] This!
Can Mischief dwell beneath this reverend Shape?
Confess who taught thee so much Cruelty.
Confess, or I will kill thee.

RODERIGO - The Cardinal.

QUEEN ISABELLA - The Cardinal!

ABDELAZER - Oh impious Traitor!
How came I mention'd then?

RODERIGO - To get Admittance.

ABDELAZER - But why do I delay thy Punishment?
Die, and be damn'd together. [Aside.]
[Stabs him.
But oh, my Queen! Elvira, call for help.
Have I remov'd all that oppos'd our Flame,
[Kneels.
To have it thus blown out, thus in a Minute?
When I, all full of youthful Fire, all Love,
Had rais'd my Soul with Hopes of near Delights,
To meet thee cold, and pale; to find those Eyes,
Those charming Eyes thus dying. Oh ye Powers!
Take all the Prospect of my future Joys,
And turn it to Despair, since thou art gone.

QUEEN ISABELLA - Cease, cease your kind Complaints, my struggling Soul,
'Twixt Death, and Love, holds an uneasy Contest;
This will not let it stay, nor that depart;
And whilst I hear thy Voice thus breathing Love,
It hovers still-about-the grateful-Sound.
My Eyes-have took-an everlasting Leave
Of all that blest their Sight; and now a gloomy Darkness
Benights the wishing Sense, that vainly strives
To take another View; but 'tis too late,
And Life and Love - must yield to Death - and
Fate.
[Dies.

ABDELAZER - Farewell, my greatest Plague,
[He rises with Joy.
Thou wert a most impolitick loving thing;
And having done my Bus'ness which thou wert born for,
'Twas time thou shouldst retire,
And leave me free to love, and reign alone.

Enter Leonora, Alonzo, Ordonio, and other Men and Women.

Come all the World, and pay your Sorrows here,
Since all the World has Interest in this Loss.

ALONZO - The Moor in Tears! nay, then the Sin was his.

LEONORA - The Queen my Mother dead!
How many Sorrows will my Heart let in,
E'er it will break in pieces.
[Weeps over her.

ALONZO - I know the Source of all this Villany,
And need not ask you how the Queen came murder'd.

ELVIRA - My Lord, that Fryer, from the Cardinal, did it.

ALONZO - The Cardinal!
'Tis possible, for the Injuries she did him
Cou'd be repaid with nothing less than Death. [Aside.
My Fair, your Griefs have been so just of late,
I dare not beg that you would weep no more;
Though every Tear those lovely Eyes let fall,
Give me a killing Wound. Remove the Body.

[Guards remove the Body. Ex. all but Alonzo and Leonora.

Such Objects suit not Souls so soft as thine.

LEONORA - With Horrors I am grown of late familiar;
I saw my Father die, and liv'd the while;
I saw my beauteous Friend, and thy lov'd Sister,
Florella, whilst her Breast was bleeding fresh;
Nay, and my Brother's too, all full of Wounds,
The best and kindest Brother that ever Maid was blest with;
Poor Philip bound, and led like Victims for a Sacrifice;
All this I saw and liv'd
And canst thou hope for Pity from that Heart,
Whose harden'd Sense is Proof 'gainst all these Miseries?
This Moor, Alonzo, is a subtle Villain,
Yet of such Power we scarce dare think him such.

ALONZO - 'Tis true, my charming Fair, he is that Villain,
As ill and powerful too; yet he has a Heart
That may be reach'd with this but 'tis not time,
[Points to his Sword.
We must dissemble yet, which is an Art
Too foul for Souls so innocent as thine.
Enter Abdelazer.
The Moor!
Hell! will he not allow us sorrowing time?

ABDELAZER - Madam, I come to pay my humblest Duty,
And know what Service you command your Slave.

LEONORA - Alas, I've no Commands; or if I had,
I am too wretched now to be obey'd.

ABDELAZER - Can one so fair, and great, ask any thing
Of Men, or Heaven, they wou'd not grant with Joy?

LEONORA - Hea'vns Will I'm not permitted to dispute,
And may implore in vain; but 'tis in you
To grant me what may yet preserve my Life.

ABDELAZER - In me! in me! the humblest of your Creatures!

By yon bright Sun, or your more splendid Eyes,
I wou'd divest my self of every Hope,
To gratify one single Wish of yours.
Name but the way.

LEONORA - I am so unhappy, that the only thing
I have to ask, is what you must deny;
The Liberty of Philip

ABDELAZER - How! Philip's Liberty and must I grant it?
I (in whose Hands Fortune had put the Crown)
Had I not lov'd the Good and Peace of Spain,
Might have dispos'd it to my own Advantage;
And shall that Peace,
Which I've preferr'd above my proper Glories,
Be lost again in him, in him a Bastard?

ALONZO - That he's a Bastard, is not, Sir, believ'd;
And she that cou'd love you, might after that
Do any other Sin, and 'twas the least
Of all the Number to declare him Bastard.

ABDELAZER - How, Sir! that you'd love me! what is there here,
Or in my Soul, or Person, may not be belov'd?

ALONZO - I spoke without Reflection on your Person,
But of dishonest Love, which was too plain,
From whence came all the Ills we have endur'd;
And now being warm in Mischiefs,
Thou dost pursue the Game, till all be thine.

ABDELAZER - Mine!

ALONZO - Yes, thine
The little humble Mask which you put on
Upon the Face of Falshood, and Ambition,
Is easily seen thro; you gave a Crown,
But you'll command the Kingly Power still,
Arm and disband, destroy or save at Pleasure.

ABDELAZER - Vain Boy, (whose highest Fame,
Is that thou art the great Alvaro's Son)
Where learnt you so much daring, to upbraid
My generous Power thus falsly, do you know me?

ALONZO - Yes, Prince, and 'tis that Knowledge makes me dare;
I know thy Fame in Arms; I know in Battels
Thou hast perform'd Deeds much above thy Years:
My Infant Courage too
(By the same Master taught) grew up to thine,
When thou in Rage out-didst me, not in Bravery.

I know thou'st greater Power too, thank thy Treachery!

ABDELAZER - Dost thou not fear that Power?

ALONZO - By Heaven, not I,
Whilst I can this command.
[Lays his Hand on his Sword.

ABDELAZER - I too command a Sword.
[Abd. lays his Hand on his, and comes close up to him.
But not to draw on thee, Alonzo;
Since I can prove thy Accusation false
By ways more grateful, take this Ring, Alonzo;
The sight of it will break down Prison-Gates,
And set all free, as was the first-born Man.

ALONZO - What means this turn?

ABDELAZER - To enlarge Philip; but on such Conditions,
As you think fit to make for my Security:
And as thou'rt brave, deal with me as I merit.

ALONZO - Art thou in earnest?

ABDELAZER - I am, by all that's sacred.

LEONORA - Oh, let me fall before you, and ne'er rise,
Till I have made you know what Gratitude
Is fit for such a Bounty!
Haste, my Alonzo, haste and treat with Philip;
Nor do I wish his Freedom, but on such Terms
As may be advantageous to the Moor.

ALONZO - Nor I, by Heaven! I know the Prince's Soul,
Though it be fierce, has Gratitude and Honour;
And for a Deed like this, will make returns,
Such as are worthy of the brave Obliger.

[Exit Alonzo.

ABDELAZER - Yes, if he be not gone to Heaven before you come. [Aside.
What will become of Abdelazer now,
Who with his Power has thrown away his Liberty?

LEONORA - Your Liberty! Oh, Heaven forbid that you,
Who can so generously give Liberty,
Should be depriv'd of it!
It must not be whilst Leonora lives.

ABDELAZER - 'Tis she that takes it from me.

LEONORA - I! Alas, I wou'd not for the World
Give you one minute's Pain.

ABDELAZER - You cannot help it, 'tis against your Will;
Your Eyes insensibly do wound and kill.

LEONORA - What can you mean? and yet I fear to know.

ABDELAZER - Most charming of your Sex! had Nature made
This clouded Face, like to my Heart, all Love,
It might have spar'd that Language which you dread;
Whose rough harsh sound, unfit for tender Ears,
Will ill express the Business of my Life.

LEONORA - Forbear it, if that Business, Sir, be Love.

ABDELAZER - Gods!
Because I want the art to tell my Story
In that soft way, which those can do whose Business
Is to be still so idly employ'd,
I must be silent and endure my Pain,
Which Heaven ne'er gave me so much lameness for.
Love in my Soul is not that gentle thing
It is in other Breasts; instead of Calms,
It ruffles mine into uneasy Storms.
I wou'd not love, if I cou'd help it, Madam;
But since 'tis not to be resisted here
You must permit it to approach your Ear.

LEONORA - Not when I cannot hear it, Sir, with Honour.

ABDELAZER - With Honour!
Nay, I can talk in the Defence of that:
By all that's sacred, 'tis a Flame as virtuous,
As every Thought inhabits your fair Soul,
And it shall learn to be as gentle too;
For I must merit you

LEONORA - I will not hear this Language; merit me!

ABDELAZER - Yes, why not?
You're but the Daughter of the King of Spain,
And I am Heir to great Abdela, Madam;
I can command this Kingdom you possess,
(Of which my Passion only made you Queen)
And re-assume that which your Father took
From mine, a Crown as bright as that of Spain.

LEONORA - You said you wou'd be gentle

ABDELAZER - I will; this sullen Heart shall learn to bow,

And keep it self within the Bounds of Love;
Its Language I'll deliver out in Sighs,
Soft as the Whispers of a yielding Virgin.
I cou'd transform my Soul to any Shape;
Nay, I could even teach my Eyes the Art
To change their natural Fierceness into Smiles;
What is't I wou'd not do to gain that Heart!

LEONORA - Which never can be yours! that and my Vows,
Are to Alonzo given; which he lays claim to
By the most sacred Ties, Love and Obedience;
All Spain esteems him worthy of that Love.

ABDELAZER - More worthy it than I! it was a Woman,
A nice, vain, peevish Creature that pronounc'd it;
Had it been Man, 't had been his last Transgression.
His Birth! his glorious Actions! are they like mine?

LEONORA - Perhaps his Birth wants those Advantages,
Which Nature has laid out in Beauty on his Person.

ABDELAZER - Ay! there's your Cause of Hate! Curst be my Birth,
And curst be Nature that has dy'd my Skin
With this ungrateful Colour! cou'd not the Gods
Have given me equal Beauty with Alonzo!
Yet as I am, I've been in vain ador'd,
And Beauties great as thine have languish'd for me.
The Lights put out, thou in thy naked Arms
Will find me soft and smooth as polish'd Ebony;
And all my Kisses on thy balmy Lips as sweet,
As are the Breezes, breath'd amidst the Groves
Of ripening Spices in the height of Day:
As vigorous too,
As if each Night were the first happy Moment
I laid thy panting Body to my Bosom.
Oh, that transporting Thought
See, I can bend as low, and sigh as often,
[Kneels.
And sue for Blessings only you can grant;
As any fair and soft Alonzo can
If you could pity me as well
But you are deaf, and in your Eyes I read
[Rises with Anger.
A Scorn which animates my Love and Anger;
Nor know I which I should dismiss or cherish.

LEONORA - The last is much more welcome than the first;
Your Anger can but kill; but, Sir, your Love
Will make me ever wretched, since 'tis impossible
I ever can return it.

ABDELAZER - Why, kill me then! you must do one or t'other.
[Kneels.
For thus, I cannot live, why dost thou weep?
Thy every Tear's enough to drown my Soul!
How tame Love renders every feeble Sense!
[Rises.
Gods! I shall turn Woman, and my Eyes inform me
The Transformation's near. Death! I'll not endure it,
I'll fly before sh'as quite undone my Soul
[Offers to go.
But 'tis not in my Power, she holds it fast
And I can now command no single part
[Returns.
Tell me, bright Maid, if I were amiable,
And you were uningag'd, could you then love me?

LEONORA - No! I could die first.

ABDELAZER - Hah! awake, my Soul, from out this drousy Fit,
And with thy wonted Bravery scorn thy Fetters.
By Heaven, 'tis gone! and I am now my self.
Be gone, my dull Submission! my lazy Flame
Grows sensible, and knows for what 'twas kindled.
Coy Mistress, you must yield, and quickly too:
Were you devout as Vestals, pure as their Fire,
Yet I wou'd wanton in the rifled Spoils
Of all that sacred Innocence and Beauty.
Oh, my Desire's grown high!
Raging as midnight Flames let loose in Cities,
And, like that too, will ruin where it lights.
Come, this Apartment was design'd for Pleasure,
And made thus silent, and thus gay for me;
There I'll convince that Error, that vainly made thee think
I was not meant for Love.

LEONORA - Am I betray'd? are all my Women gone?
And have I nought but Heaven for my Defence?

ABDELAZER - None else, and that's too distant to befriend you.

LEONORA - Oh, take my Life, and spare my dearer Honour!
Help, help, ye Powers that favour Innocence.
[Enter Women.
Just as the Moor is going to force in Leonora,
enters to him Osmin in haste.

OSMIN - My Lord, Alonzo

ABDELAZER - What of him, you Slave, is he not secur'd?
Speak, dull Intruder, that know'st not times and seasons,
Or get thee hence.

OSMIN - Not till I've done the Business which I came for.

ABDELAZER - Slave! that thou cam'st for.
[Stabs him in the Arm.

OSMIN - No, 'twas to tell you, that Alonzo,
Finding himself betray'd, made brave resistance;
Some of your Slaves h'as killed, and some h'as wounded.

ABDELAZER - 'Tis time he were secured;
I must assist my Guards, or all is lost.
[Exit.

LEONORA - Sure, Osmin, from the Gods thou cam'st,
To hinder my undoing; and if thou dy'st,
Heaven will almost forgive thy other Sins
For this one pious Deed.
But yet I hope thy Wound's not mortal.

OSMIN - 'Tis only in my Arm and, Madam, for this pity,
I'll live to do you Service.

LEONORA - What Service can the Favourite of the Moor,
Train'd up in Blood and Mischiefs, render me?

OSMIN - Why, Madam, I command the Guard of Moors,
Who will all die, when e'er I give the Word.
Madam, 'twas I caus'd Philip and the Cardinal
To fly to th' Camp,
And gave 'em warning of approaching Death.

LEONORA - Heaven bless thee for thy Goodness.

OSMIN - I am weary now of being a Tyrant's Slave,
And bearing Blows too; the rest I could have suffer'd.
Madam, I'll free the Prince.
But see, the Moor returns.

LEONORA - That Monster's Presence I must fly, as from a killing Plague.

[Ex. with her Women.
Enter Abdelazer with Zarrack, and a Train of Moors.

ABDELAZER - It is prodigious, that a single Man
Should with such Bravery defend his Life
Amongst so many Swords; but he is safe.
Osmin, I am not us'd to sue for Pardon,
And when I do, you ought to grant it me.

OSMIN - I did not merit, Sir, so harsh a Usage.

ABDELAZER - No more; I'm asham'd to be upbraided,
And will repair the Injury I did thee.

OSMIN - Acknowledgment from you is pay sufficient.

ABDELAZER - Yet, Osmin, I shou'd chide your Negligence,
Since by it Philip lives still, and the Cardinal.

OSMIN - I had design'd it, Sir, this Evening's Sacrifice.

ABDELAZER - Zarrack shall now perform it and instantly:
Alonzo too must bear 'em company.

ZARRACK - I'll shew my Duty in my haste, my Lord.
[Ex. Zarrack.

OSMIN - Death! I'm undone; I'll after him, and kill him.
[Offers to go.

ABDELAZER - Osmin, I've business with you.

[Osmin comes back bowing.

As they are going off, enter Leonora, Ordonio, other Lords, and Women.

LEONORA - Oh Prince! for Pity hear and grant my Suit.
[Kneels.

ABDELAZER - When so much Beauty's prostrate at my Feet,
What is't I can deny? rise, thou brightest Virgin
That ever Nature made;
Rise, and command my Life, my Soul, my Honour.

LEONORA - No, let me hang for ever on your Knees,
Unless you'll grant Alonzo Liberty.

ABDELAZER - Rise, I will grant it; though Alonzo, Madam,
Betray'd that Trust I had repos'd in him.

LEONORA - I know there's some Mistake; let me negotiate
Between my Brother and the Gallant Moor.
I cannot force your Guards,
There is no Danger in a Woman's Arm.

ABDELAZER - In your bright Eyes there is, that may corrupt 'em more
Than all the Treasures of the Eastern Kings.
Yet, Madam, here I do resign my Power;
Act as you please, dismiss Alonzo's Chains.
And since you are so generous, to despise
This Crown, which I have given you,

Philip shall owe his Greatness to your Bounty,
And whilst he makes me safe, shall rule in Spain.
Osmin -
[Whispers.

ORDONIO - And will you trust him, Madam?

LEONORA - If he deceive me, 'tis more happy far
To die with them, than live where he inhabits.

OSMIN - It shall be done.

ABDELAZER - Go, Osmin, wait upon the Queen;
And when she is confin'd, I'll visit her,
Where if she yield, she reigns; if not, she dies. [Aside.

[Ex. Abdelazer one way, Leonora, Osmin and the rest another.

SCENE III. A Prison.

Discovers Philip chain'd to a Post, and over against him the Cardinal and Alonzo in Chains.

PHILIP - Oh, all ye cruel Powers! is't not enough
I am depriv'd of Empire, and of Honour?
Have my bright Name stol'n from me, with my Crown!
Divested of all Power! all Liberty!
And here am chain'd like the sad Andromede,
To wait Destruction from the dreadful Monster!
Is not all this enough, without being damn'd,
To have thee, Cardinal, in my full view?
If I cou'd reach my Eyes, I'd be reveng'd
On the officious and accursed Lights,
For guiding so much torment to my Soul.

CARDINAL MENDOZO - My much wrong'd Prince! you need not wish to kill
By ways more certain, than by upbraiding me
With my too credulous, shameful past misdeeds.

PHILIP - If that wou'd kill, I'd weary out my Tongue
With an eternal repetition of thy Treachery;
Nay, and it shou'd forget all other Language,
But Traitor! Cardinal! which I wou'd repeat,
Till I had made my self as raging mad,
As the wild Sea, when all the Winds are up;
And in that Storm, I might forget my Grief.

CARDINAL MENDOZO - Wou'd I cou'd take the killing Object from your Eyes.

PHILIP - Oh Alonzo, to add to my Distraction,

Must I find thee a sharer in my Fate?

ALONZO - It is my Duty, Sir, to die with you.
But, Sir, my Princess
Has here a more than equal claim to Grief;
And Fear for her dear Safety will deprive me
Of this poor Life, that shou'd have been your Sacrifice.

Enter Zarrack with a Dagger; gazes on Philip.

PHILIP - Kind Murderer, welcome! quickly free my Soul,
And I will kiss the sooty Hand that wounds me.

ZARRACK - Oh, I see you can be humble.

PHILIP - Humble! I'll be as gentle as a Love-sick Youth,
When his dear Conqu'ress sighs a Hope into him,
If thou wilt kill me! Pity me and kill me.

ZARRACK - I hope to see your own Hand do that Office.

PHILIP - Oh, thou wert brave indeed,
If thou wou'dst lend me but the use of one.

ZARRACK - You'll want a Dagger then.

PHILIP - By Heaven, no, I'd run it down my Throat,
Or strike my pointed Fingers through my Breast.

ZARRACK - Ha, ha, ha, what pity 'tis you want a Hand.

Enter Osmin.

PHILIP - Osmin, sure thou wilt be so kind to kill me!
Thou hadst a Soul was humane.

OSMIN - Indeed I will not, Sir, you are my King.
[Unbinds him.

PHILIP - What mean'st thou?

OSMIN - To set you free, my Prince.

PHILIP - Thou art some Angel sure, in that dark Cloud.

ZARRACK - What mean'st thou, Traitor?

OSMIN - Wait till your Eyes inform you.

CARDINAL MENDOZO - Good Gods! what mean'st thou?

OSMIN - Sir, arm your Hand with this.
[Gives Philip a Sword, goes to undo Alonzo.

ZARRACK - Thou art half-damn'd for this!
I'll to my Prince

PHILIP - I'll stop you on your way, lie there your Tongue
[Kills him.
Shall tell no Tales to day. Now, Cardinal but hold,
I scorn to strike thee whilst thou art unarm'd,
Yet so thou didst to me;
For which I have not leisure now to kill thee.
Here, take thy Liberty; nay, do not thank me;
By Heaven, I do not mean it as a Grace.

OSMIN - My Lord, take this
[To Alonzo and the Cardinal.
And this to arm your Highness.

ALONZO - Thou dost amaze me!

OSMIN - Keep in your Wonder with your Doubts, my Lord.

PHILIP - We cannot doubt, whilst we're thus fortify'd
[Looks on his Sword.
Come, Osmin, let us fall upon the Guards.

OSMIN - There are no Guards, great Sir, but what are yours;
And see, your Friends I've brought to serve ye too.

[Opens a back Door.
Enter Leonora and Women, Ordonio, Sebastian, Antonio, etc.

PHILIP - My dearest Sister safe!

LEONORA - Whilst in your Presence, Sir, and you thus arm'd.

OSMIN - The Moor approaches, now be ready all.

PHILIP - That Name I never heard with Joy till now;
Let him come on, and arm'd with all his Powers,
Thus singly I defy him. [Draws.

Enter Abdelazer.
[Osmin secures the Doors.

ABDELAZER - Hah! betray'd! and by my Slaves! by Osmin too!

PHILIP - Now, thou damn'd Villain! true-born Soul of Hell!
Not one of thy infernal Kin shall save thee.

ABDELAZER - Base Coward Prince!
Whom the admiring World mistakes for Brave;
When all thy boasted Valour, fierce and hot
As was thy Mother in her height of Lust,
Can with the aid of all these treacherous Swords,
Take but a single Life; but such a Life,
As amongst all their Store the envying Gods
Have not another such to breathe in Man.

PHILIP - Vaunt on, thou monstrous Instrument of Hell!
For I'm so pleas'd to have thee in my Power,
That I can hear thee number up thy Sins,
And yet be calm, whilst thou art near Damnation.

ABDELAZER - Thou ly'st, thou canst not keep thy Temper in;
For hadst thou so much Bravery of Mind,
Thou'dst fight me singly; which thou dar'st not do.

PHILIP - Not dare!
By Heaven, if thou wert twenty Villains more,
And I had all thy Weight of Sins about me,
I durst thus venture on; forbear, Alonzo.

ALONZO - I will not, Sir.

PHILIP - I was indeed too rash; 'tis such a Villain,
As shou'd receive his Death from nought but Slaves.

ABDELAZER - Thou'st Reason, Prince! nor can they wound my Body
More than I've done thy Fame; for my first step
To my Revenge, I whor'd the Queen thy Mother.

PHILIP - Death! though this I knew before, yet the hard Word
Runs harshly thro my Heart;
If thou hadst murder'd fifty Royal Ferdinands,
And with inglorious Chains as many Years
Had loaded all my Limbs, 't had been more pardonable
Than this eternal Stain upon my Name:
Oh, thou hast breath'd thy worst of Venom now.

ABDELAZER - My next advance was poisoning of thy Father.

PHILIP - My Father poison'd! and by thee, thou Dog!
Oh, that thou hadst a thousand Lives to lose,
Or that the World depended on thy single one,
That I might make a Victim
Worthy to offer up to his wrong'd Ghost.
But stay, there's something of thy Count of Sins untold,
That I must know; not that I doubt, by Heaven,
That I am Philip's Son

ABDELAZER - Not for thy Ease, but to declare my Malice,
Know, Prince, I made thy amorous Mother
Proclaim thee Bastard, when I miss'd of killing rhee.

PHILIP - Gods! let me contain my Rage!

ABDELAZER - I made her too betray the credulous Cardinal,
And having then no farther use of her,
Satiated with her Lust,
I set Roderigo on to murder her.
Thy Death had next succeeded; and thy Crown
I wou'd have laid at Leonora's Feet.

ALONZO - How! durst you love the Princess?

ABDELAZER - Fool, durst! had I been born a Slave,
I durst with this same Soul do any thing:
Yes, and the last Sense that will remain about me,
Will be my Passion for that charming Maid,
Whom I'd enjoy'd e'er now, but for thy Treachery.
[To Osmin.

PHILIP - Deflour'd my Sister! Heaven punish me eternally,
If thou out-liv'st the Minute thou'st declar'd it.

ABDELAZER - I will, in spite of all that thou canst do.
Stand off, fool-hardy Youth, if thou'dst be safe,
And do not draw thy certain Ruin on,
Or think that e'er this Hand was arm'd in vain.

PHILIP - Poor angry Slave, how I contemn thee now!

ABDELAZER - As humble Huntsmen do the generous Lion;
Now thou darst see me lash my Sides, and roar,
And bite my Snare in vain; who with one Look
(Had I been free) hadst shrunk into the Earth,
For shelter from my Rage:
And like that noble Beast, though thus betray'd,
I've yet an awful Fierceness in my Looks,
Which makes thee fear t'approach; and 'tis at distance
That thou dar'st kill me; for come but in my reach,
And with one Grasp I wou'd confound thy Hopes.

PHILIP - I'll let thee see how vain thy Boastings are,
And unassisted, by one single Rage,
Thus make an easy Passage to thy Heart.

[Runs on him, all the rest do the like in the same Minute.
Abd. aims at the Prince, and kills Osmin, and falls
dead himself.

Die with thy Sins unpardon'd, and forgotten

[Shout within.

ALONZO - Great Sir, your Throne and Kingdom want you now;
Your People rude with Joy, do fill each Street,
And long to see their King, whom Heaven preserve.

ALL - Long live Philip, King of Spain

PHILIP - I thank ye all; and now, my dear Alonzo,
Receive the Recompence of all thy Sufferings,
Whilst I create thee Duke of Salamancha.

ALONZO - Thus low I take the Bounty from your Hands.
[Kneels.

LEONORA - Rise, Sir, my Brother now has made us equal.

CARDINAL MENDOZO - And shall this joyful Day, that has restor'd you
To all the Glories of your Birth and Merits,
That has restor'd all Spain the greatest Treasure
That ever happy Monarchy possess'd,
Leave only me unhappy, when, Sir, my Crime
Was only too much Faith? Thus low I fall, [Kneels.
And from that Store of Mercy Heaven has given you,
Implore you wou'd dispense a little here.

PHILIP - Rise, (though with much ado) I will forgive you.

LEONORA - Come, my dear Brother, to that glorious business,
Our Birth and Fortunes call us, let us haste,
For here methinks we are in danger still.

PHILIP - So after Storms, the joyful Mariner
Beholds the distant wish'd-for Shore afar,
And longs to bring the rich-fraight Vessel in,
Fearing to trust the faithless Seas again.

EPILOGUE.

Spoken by little Mrs. Ariell.

With late Success being blest, I'm come agen;
You see what Kindness can do, Gentlemen,
Which when once shewn, our Sex cannot refrain.
Yet spite of such a Censure I'll proceed,
And for our Poetess will intercede:
Before, a Poet's wheedling Words prevail'd,

Whose melting Speech my tender Heart assail'd,
And I the flatt'ring Scribler's Cause maintain'd;
So by my means the Fop Applauses gain'd.
'Twas wisely done to chuse m' his Advocate,
Since I have prov'd to be his better Fate;
For what I lik'd, I thought you could not hate.
Respect for you, Gallants, made me comply,
Though I confess he did my Passion try,
And I am too good-natur'd to deny.
But now not Pity, but my Sex's Cause,
Whose Beauty does, like Monarchs, give you Laws,
Should now command, being join'd with Wit, Applause.
Yet since our Beauty's Power's not absolute,
She'll not the Privilege of your Sex dispute,
But does by me submit. Yet since you've been
For my sake kind, repeat it once agen.
Your Kindness, Gallants, I shall soon repay,
If you'll but favour my Design to Day:
Your last Applauses, like refreshing Showers,
Made me spring up and bud like early Flow'rs;
Since then I'm grown at least an Inch in height,
And shall e'er long be full-blown for Delight.

Written by a Friend.

Aphra Behn – A Short Biography

Aphra Behn was baptised on December 14th in 1640.

Although she was a prolific and well established writer in her own lifetime facts about her remain scant and difficult to confirm. What can safely be said though is that Aphra Behn is now regarded as a key English playwright and a major figure in Restoration theatre

In fact even where and to whom she was born are subject to discussion.

According to which account you read – and there are many – Aphra was born in Harbledown, near Canterbury. Another that she was born to a barber, John Amis and his wife Amy. Or again she was born to a couple named Cooper.

In the "The Histories And Novels of the Late Ingenious Mrs. Behn" (1696) it is written that Aphra was born to Bartholomew Johnson, a barber, and Elizabeth Denham, a wet-nurse. However a claim by Colonel Thomas Colepeper, who states he knew her as a child, wrote in Adversaria that she was born at "Sturry or Canterbury" to a Mr Johnson and that she had a sister named Frances. Anne Kingsmill Finch, Countess of Winchilsea, a poetic contemporary, says that Aphra was born in Wye in Kent, and was the 'Daughter to a Barber.'

None of these accounts can be relied upon and it follows that with so few facts the early part of her life cannot be clearly illustrated.

However what can be accurately suggested is that Aphra was born in the rising tensions to the English Civil War. Obviously a time of much division and difficulty as the King and Parliament, and their respective forces, came ever closer to conflict.

But still facts do not reveal themselves in any quantity. As a young woman a version exists of Aphra's journeying to Surinam with Bartholomew Johnson. He was said to have died on the journey, leaving his wife and children spending some months in the country. It is during this trip that Aphra claims to have met an African slave leader. These experiences formed the basis for one of her most famous works, "Oroonoko". In "Oroonoko" Behn Aphra gifts herself the position of narrator and her first biographer accepted the proposition that Aphra was indeed the daughter of the lieutenant general of Surinam, as in the story. There is little evidence to support this case, and none of her contemporaries acknowledge this, or any, aristocratic status. There is also no evidence that Oroonoko existed as an actual person or that any such slave revolt, is anything but an invention.

However it is possible that she acted a spy in the colony. Possibilities exist. Perhaps Aphra re-wrote her own history as and when it suited her needs at the time.

The common method of gathering information in these times was Church records and for a few, tax records. Aphra Behn is mentioned in neither. As well as Aphra Behn or Mrs Behn she was, at times, also known as Ann Behn, Mrs Bean, agent 160 and Astrea.

Shortly after her supposed return to England from Surinam in 1664, Aphra may have married Johan Behn (also written as Johann and John Behn). He could have been a merchant of German or Dutch extraction, possibly from Hamburg. He died or the couple separated that same year, however from this point we can be sure Aphra used the title "Mrs Behn" as her professional name.

There is some suggestion that Aphra may have been a Catholic or at least leaned towards this school of faith. She once commented that she was "designed for a nun." Many of those around her were Catholic, such as Henry Neville who was later arrested for his Catholicism, and this would have aroused suspicions during the anti-Catholic fervour of the 1680s. She was a monarchist, and her sympathy for the Stuarts, and particularly for the Catholic Duke of York may be demonstrated by her dedication of her play "The Rover, Part II" to him after he had been exiled for the second time. Aphra was dedicated to the restored King Charles II. As political parties emerged during this time, Aphra became a Tory supporter.

By 1666 Aphra had become attached to the court. Domestically the Plague was sweeping the Nation and the Great Fire was about to erupt through London. In foreign affairs England and the Netherlands had engaged in The Second Anglo-Dutch War from 1665. Aphra was recruited as a political spy in Antwerp on behalf of King Charles II, possibly in league with Thomas Killigrew.

This is probably the beginning of more accurate records on Aphra's life. Her code name is said to have been Astrea (though there are others), a name under which she later published many of her writings. Her chief duty was to establish a relationship with William Scot, son of Thomas Scot, a regicide who had been executed in 1660. Scot was believed to be ready to become a spy in the English service and to report on the activities of the English exiles who were thought to be plotting against the King. Aphra arrived in Bruges in July 1666 with a mission to secure Scot into a double agent, but there is evidence that Scot would betray her to the Dutch.

Aphra however found life as a spy not quite the romantic interlude that many assume would be the case. She arrived unprepared; the cost of living shocked her, and after a month, she had to pawn her jewellery. King Charles was slow in paying, either for her services or for her expenses whilst abroad.

She had to borrow money so she could return to London, where she spent a year petitioning King Charles for payment unsuccessfully. A short while later a warrant was issued for her arrest, but little to suggest it was actually served or that she went to prison for her debt.

The death of her husband and her debts seemed to push her towards a more sustainable and substantial career. Aphra began work for the King's Company and the Duke's Company players as a scribe. These were, in fact, the only two licensed theatre groups in London. The theatres had been closed under Cromwell and were now re-opening under Charles II and a more liberal atmosphere. Theatre technology was being imported from Europe and being integrated into the staging of some plays. It was a great moment on which to embark upon a career in theatre.

Aphra who had previously only written poetry now embarked on such a career. Her first, "The Forc'd Marriage", was staged in 1670, followed by "The Amorous Prince" (1671). After her third play, "The Dutch Lover", fails to please Aphra had a three year lull in her writing career. Again it is speculated that she went travelling again, possibly once again as a spy.

After this sojourn her writing moves towards comic works, which prove commercially more successful. Her most popular works included "The Rover" and "Love-Letters Between a Nobleman and His Sister" (1684–87).

With her growing reputation Aphra became friends with many of the most notable writers of the day. This is The Age of Dryden and his literary dominance. As well as his friendship she includes also those of Elizabeth Barry, John Hoyle, Thomas Otway and Edward Ravenscroft, and was also attached to the circle of the Earl of Rochester.

Aphra often used her plays to attack the parliamentary Whigs claiming, "In public spirits call'd, good o' th' Commonwealth... So tho' by different ways the fever seize...in all 'tis one and the same mad disease." This was Aphra's criticism to parliament which had denied the king funds.

From the mid 1680's Aphra's health began to decline. This was exacerbated by her continual state of debt and descent into poverty.

In 1687 she published A Discovery of New Worlds, a translation of a French popularisation of astronomy, Entretiens sur la pluralité des mondes, by Bernard le Bovier de Fontenelle, written as a novel in a form similar to her own work, but with her new, religiously oriented preface.

As her end approached in 1689 it became increasingly hard for her to even hold a pen though her desire to continue to write was unquenchable. In her final days, she wrote the translation of the final book of Abraham Cowley's Six Books of Plants.

Aphra Behn died on April 16th 1689, and is buried in the East Cloister of Westminster Abbey. The inscription on her tombstone reads: "Here lies a Proof that Wit can never be Defence enough against Mortality." She was quoted as stating that she had led a "life dedicated to pleasure and poetry."

Her legacy is broad. Firstly as a woman she broke down many of the barriers which regarded only men as writers, especially in the commercial arena. In all she would write and have performed 19 plays, contribute to more, and become one of the first prolific, high-profile female dramatists in these Isles.

In her own golden age of the 1670s and 1680s she was one of the most productive playwrights in Britain, second only to the immense talents of the Poet Laureate John Dryden.

Much of her work has been criticised for its bawdy tone as well as its masculine form but needs must and she was working to live, to survive, and to widen her spread as an author.

She received widespread support from many other successful writers including Thomas Otway, Nahum Tate (also a Poet Laureate), Jacob Tonson, Nathaniel Lee and Thomas Creech.

Aphra is now rightly seen as a key dramatist of the seventeenth-century theatre. Her prose vitally important to the on-going development of the English novel.

Following Aphra's death new female dramatists such as 'Ariadne', Delarivier Manley, Mary Fix, Susanna Centlivre and Catherine Trotter acknowledged Behn as an inspiration who opened up the public space for women writers to be accepted.

In succeeding centuries her appreciation has been volatile. For instance in the morally reserved Victorian clime both the writer and her works were ignored or dismissed as indecent. The Victorian novelist and critic Julia Kavanagh wrote, "the disgrace of Aphra Behn is that, instead of raising man to woman's moral standard, she sank woman to the level of man's coarseness".

However by the 20th century, however, Aphra's fame was back in fashion. Since then her works have been well appreciated and her place in our literary pantheon assured.

Aphra Behn – A Concise Bibliography

Plays

The Forced Marriage (1670)
The Amorous Prince (1671)
The Dutch Lover (1673)
Abdelazer (1676)
The Town Fop (1676)
The Rover, Part I (1677)
Sir Patient Fancy (1678)
The Feigned Courtesans (1679)
The Young King (1679)
The False Count (1681)
The Rover, Part II (1681)
The Roundheads (1681)
The City Heiress (1682)
Like Father, Like Son (1682)
Prologue and Epilogue to Romulus and Hersilia, or The Sabine War (November 1682)
The Lucky Chance (1686) with composer John Blow
The Emperor of the Moon (1687)
The Widow Ranter (1689)
The Younger Brother (1696)

Novels

The Fair Jilt
Agnes de Castro
Love-Letters Between a Nobleman and His Sister (1684)

Oroonoko (1688)

Short Stories

The Fair Jilt (1688)
The History of the Nun: or, the Fair Vow-Breaker (1688)
The History of the Servant
The Lover-Boy of Germany
The Girl Who Loved the German Lover-Boy

Poetry Collections

Poems upon Several Occasions, with A Voyage to the Island of Love (1684)
Lycidus; or, The Lover in Fashion (1688)

The Dorset Square Theatre – A Short History

Many of Aphra Behn's plays were first performed at the Dorset Garden Theatre in London which was originally built in 1671.

The theatre itself is rich in history though it survived for less than forty years. In its first years it was also commonly called the Duke of York's Theatre, as well as the Duke's Theatre. Charles II died in 1685 and his brother the Duke of York was crowned King James II. The theatre then changed its name to The Queen's Theatre in honour of James' wife Mary of Modena.

It was the fourth home of the Duke's Company, one of the two patent theatre companies in Restoration London, and after 1682 continued to be used by the company's successor, the United Company.

After the Civil war and the harsh years of the Interregnum the ban on theatres was lifted with the Restoration of Charles II in 1660. He granted Letters Patent to two theatre companies. One enjoyed his own patronage, this was 'The King's Company'. The other was patronised by his brother the Duke of York and was known as The Duke's Company.

Both were originally based in the Cockpit Theatre, an old Jacobean theatre in Drury Lane. The Duke's Company then moved for a short time to the Salisbury Court Theatre and thence in 1662 to Portugal Street in Lincoln's Inn Fields remaining there until 1671. The King's Company meanwhile moved to the Theatre Royal, Drury Lane.

Sir William Davenant, the respected Poet Laureate, founded the Duke's company and brought much innovation to theatre especially with regard to changeable scenery and theatrical machinery.

Davenant died on April 7th 1668. He had made plans for a new theatre but died before ground was broken on the new theatre in 1670. This was funded to the tune of £9,000 by the Davenant family, the theatre's leading actor Thomas Betterton and others. A site was leased in Dorset Square under a 39 year lease at a rent of £130.55 per annum.

The theatre opened in the following year with the return of Thomas Betterton to England from a trip to France. It is thought that Betterton had gone several times over the years to bring back French thinking and equipment and certainly this seems evident with the Company's elaborate productions, including operatic adaptations of Shakespeare's Macbeth (1673), The Tempest (1674), and Thomas Shadwell's Pysche (1675). These productions employed changeable perspective scenery moved by machines as well as for flying actors and objects

The site of the theatre, was in the former grounds of Dorset House, London seat of the Sackville Earls of Dorset. Destroyed in the Great Fire of London it was soon densely built over with speculative tenements. It appears part of the site had been used as a theatre in the time of Charles I: in 1629 the Earl of Dorset leased the "stables and out howses towards the water side" behind Dorset House... to make a playhouse for the children of the revels."

The site for the new theatre, by Dorset Stairs in Whitefriars on the Thames, was slightly upstream from the outlet of the New Canal, part of the Fleet River. Its position on the Thames permitted the patrons to travel to the theatre by boat, avoiding the nearby crime-ridden neighbourhood of Alsatia.

It opened on 9 November 1671 and was almost twice the size of the Duke's Company's former theatre. It became the principal playhouse in London when the Theatre Royal burned down in January 1672, and only rivalled when the new Theatre Royal opened in March 1674.

After the Duke's Company merged with the King's Company in 1682 to form the United Company, the theatre in Dorset Garden was used mainly for opera, music, and spectaculars. From the 1690s it was used as well for other entertainments, such as weight lifting, until it was demolished in 1709.

Apart from the illustrations in the libretto of The Empress of Morocco, no contemporary pictures of the interior are known. It is thought that the interior was richly decorated: the proscenium arch had carvings by Grinling Gibbons.

The Dorset Garden theatre, typically for English theatres, had a large forestage. Edward Langhans in his reconstruction calculated the forestage to be 19'6" feet deep and 30'6" wide at the proscenium arch. This forestage provided actors, singers and dancers with a sizeable downstage and a well lit performance space, free of grooves. When a locale was depicted by the scenery, the forestage was understood to be an extension of that place and served as the link between the audience and the performers, the auditorium and the stage, the playgoers and the play.

Access to the forestage was by proscenium doors, probably two on each side of the stage. Above the doors were balconies; acting spaces that could also serve for seating.

The scenic stage was probably some 50' deep and 30' high. The proscenium arch may have been some 30' wide and at least 25' high to accommodate the scenery in operas such as Dioclesian, The Fairy-Queen, or The World in the Moon. Both the forestage and the scenic stage were raked.

The music box above the proscenium arch could hold perhaps 8 to 10 musicians, to provide incidental music. A full orchestra would be sitting in the pit, just in front of the stage.

The Duke's Company had already been using moveable scenery to good effect in their previous playhouses. It was first employed by Davenant at Rutland House, using shutters in grooves, which could be slid open or closed to reveal a new scene. However Dorset Garden was also equipped to fly at least four separate people and large objects like a cloud covering the full width of the stage and carrying a large group of musicians (such as in Psyche 1675). There were also numerous floor traps.

It was primarily designed for staging Restoration spectaculars, and was the only playhouse in London capable of all the effects these lavish and exuberant spectacles required.

It is not known who designed the new theatre building. On the outside it measured 148' by 57', including a 10' deep porch.

A foreign visitor reported in 1676 that it contained a central "pit", in the form of an amphitheatre, two tiers of seven boxes each holding twenty people, and an upper gallery. In all the theatre could entertain 850 people at a time. The theatre represented a great investment to the Duke's Company.

Thomas Betterton lived in an apartment on an upper floor on the south side. And living nearby were such luminaries as Aphra Behn in Dorset Street; John Dryden in Salisbury Square (from 1673 to 1682) and John Locke in Dorset Court in 1690.

www.ingramcontent.com/pod-product-compliance
Lightning Source LLC
LaVergne TN
LVHW020652100826
845148LV00012B/2454

* 9 7 8 1 7 8 5 4 3 1 6 5 4 *